fatherP♂WER®

Generational Leadership

DON WOOD

Cover design and layout ~ Bruce Forgan (www.bdfdesignworks.com)
Author Photographs ~ Jay Young (www.jayyoung.com)

Fatherpower®*– Generational Leadership*
ISBN-13: 978-0-9745377-0-2
ISBN-10: 0-9745377-0-5

MPower Publishing
P.O. Box 1201
Bedford, Texas 76095-1201

www.fatherpower.com

Fatherpower® is a registered trademark.

Printed in the United States of America.

Introducing
Don Wood and FATHERPOWER®

"At a time when our nation is full of fatherless families, finally somebody speaks about the power of a father. This compelling book will change your life."

Chuck Brewster, U.S. Secret Service Agent, Retired;
Former National Director, HonorBound-Men of
Promise; Founder and President, Champions of Honor

"This is the hour for the release of FATHERPOWER®! Don Wood has written how to restore the power into natural and spiritual fatherhood. This is a great read and a great study book."

John P. Kelly, President, Leadership Education for
Advancement and Development; International
Coalition of Apostles

"Don't read this book ... live it. Close yourself away, capture time to feel the warmth of this story ... as enduring as the universe, as comforting as your secret place ... the loving embrace of a God who passionately loves you. Don Wood captures the textures, joys, and hurts real families are made of ... and then shows us how to find our way into the extravagant love of a wonderful father, Almighty God. Don't just read this book, enjoy the journey for yourself ... here is what life is all about. You've found a precious gem!"

Paul Cole, President, Christian Men's Network;
Pastor, Hope Christian City Church,
Colleyville, Texas

"My wife and I read three chapters of your book, wept, and rejoiced at the wonderful stories. Thank you so much."

Louie Kaupp, Staff Pastor, Eagle's Nest Christian
Fellowship, San Antonio, Texas

"Outside of Jesus, perhaps the one significant person who has impacted my relationship with my family as a father is Don Wood. ... Every husband and father should be required to attend one of his seminars before being allowed to have children. RARELY does anybody come up with anything really different that I am impressed with. Don's teaching on FATHERHOOD is both different and EXCELLENT!"

Dr. Marvin Perkins, *Paraclete*, Holy Spirit Special Interest Group, MENSA, May 1995

"I am pleased to recommend Don Wood. Seasoned by many battles, he's passionate about his 'Restoration of Fatherhood' message, both encouraging and inspirational."

Dr. Karl D. Strader, Pastor, Carpenter's Home Church, Lakeland, Florida

"I just read the chapter on Blessing. That is good stuff. Very powerful. It needs to spread."

Marie Novocin, Home School Parent

"I read FATHERPOWER® two years ago for personal devotions. It changed my life! Its wisdom helped me evaluate my actions as a parent and brought me to a new respect for my husband's gifted "fatherpower." A little book on fathering improved a marriage! I saw in practice the principles this book enjoyably and cleverly teaches. Impressed with its implications on the child, I passed copies around the campus to key individuals."

Kathy Bucklew, Registrar, Southeastern University, Lakeland, Florida

"When I got off track and things seemed hopeless, Don's message never changed. He kept telling me to work on my relationship with God. His message of a Father's heart has totally changed how I relate to everyone around me. I know that Don Wood and FATHERPOWER® were the instruments God used to bring me into His Kingdom and join me to His work."

Don Wilburn, Businessman

"I have never enjoyed being 'preached at,' whether from a pulpit or the pages of a book. Perhaps that is why I really enjoy Don Wood and FATHERPOWER®. Don brings great practical and scriptural insight to the 'job' of fathering with such humor and wisdom that you never realize you are being taught. As you read, you find your own life and experiences being remembered, reflected, and, perhaps for the first time, clearly understood. Don teaches by Scripture, anecdote, and revelatory truth. FATHERPOWER® is not just a good read—it's a 'God read!'"

William (Bill) Tome, President, Omni Medical Management Systems, Inc.

"I've known the Wood family for years. Mark, the oldest of the four sons, is my best friend and a cast of his father. My faith was poorly defined. I knew there was a God, but I didn't know Him. The Wood family prayers have a business partner familiarity—as though God is in the chair next to them at a corporate meeting—prayers so powerful they brought this sinner back to a relationship with God. Don has God's blessing and therefore mine."

Josh Massey, President, Homeland Distributing; Chief Flight Instructor; Real Estate Entrepreneur

PREFACE

Fatherhood or the lack of it powerfully impacts culture—home, business, and government. There is no greater social force than fatherhood; its power unites or alienates generations. The origin of good fatherhood is God—"For this reason I bow my knees before the Father, from whom every family ("patriarchy" in the original Greek text) in heaven and earth derives its name" Ephesians 3:14, 15.

Fatherhood derives its name, nature, and function from God, our Heavenly Father. God is not an impersonal force. On the throne of the universe—with all power, all knowledge, all creativity—is a **Father,** a Father who loves us, who plans to involve us in His epic adventure!

Natural fathers in homes, spiritual "fathers" in churches, and business "fathers" in the marketplace have a responsibility to exercise their office in a godly manner. The greater the authority, the greater the care required in exercising it. **As with Jesus and His Father, real fathers are usually invisible when their kids are on stage.** Authority exercised with a father's heart is that of a servant, promoting the next generation.

From childhood, we are imprinted with an image of fatherhood—from parents, ministers, bosses, even government leaders. This strongly affects our relationship with God. If the image is negative, we can struggle for years unless we receive revelation about who God is—our Heavenly Father.

Jesus told parables—stories—to teach truth and reveal His relationship with God, His Heavenly Father.

I love stories. The "father stories" in this book present principles of fatherhood that are eternal, effective, self-reproducing, and applicable to everyone. They reveal the heart of the Father. Understanding fatherhood unlocks secrets of the Kingdom of God that affect our whole life. **Embracing that revelation reveals who we are—we discover our true identity.**

Leadership begins with fatherhood. Learning about fatherhood from the ultimate Father will benefit you and everyone around you. Join the adventure! Allow our Father to draw you close to Him as you read *Fatherpower—Generational Leadership*.

"For I know the plans I have for you," declares the Lord, "plans to prosper you and not to harm you, plans to give you hope and a future" Jeremiah 29:11 NIV.

~ *Don Wood*, a father

TABLE OF CONTENTS

PART ONE

RECEIVING
IMPARTATION

1

Evangel WORLD PRAYER CENTER

Talk about this mom teaching them to pray out loud. Mom GOT TB AND THEY PRAYD until She was healed.

Mom had no idea she would be the first beneficiary of teaching us to pray!

Do you have A STORY ABOUT How GOD ANSERED YOUR PRAYER.

Adventures in Prayer

I t didn't start with Dad—he was the provider but not the spiritual leader. Mom taught us to pray. She imparted something to us boys. It stuck with us. It worked. It ultimately blessed her as well as Dad.

"It is no secret, what God can do. What He's done for others, He'll do for you," sang Red Foley as his voice, over the radio, filled our home. It was the early 1950s. Mom was instructing us to **always pray and never give up**—**"Nothing is impossible with God,"** she said. She had no idea her little boys would soon have to apply what she was teaching them or that she would benefit so dramatically.

Many times she shared with us Psalm 91, her favorite Scripture passage. It seemed to suit the atmosphere around her—praying, believing God in hard circumstances, needing God's help so frequently:

> He who dwells in the shelter of the Most High will abide in the shadow of the Almighty. I will say to the Lord, 'My refuge and my fortress, my God, in whom I trust!' For it is He who delivers you from the snare of the trapper,

and from the deadly pestilence. He will cover you with His pinions, and under His wings you may seek refuge; His faithfulness is a shield and bulwark. You will not be afraid of the terror by night, or of the arrow that flies by day; of the pestilence that stalks in darkness, or of the destruction that lays waste at noon. A thousand may fall at your side, and ten thousand at your right hand; but it shall not approach you. You will only look on with your eyes, and see the recompense of the wicked.

For you have made the Lord, my refuge, even the Most High, your dwelling place. No evil will befall you, nor will any plague come near your tent. For He will give His angels charge concerning you, to guard you in all your ways. They will bear you up in their hands, lest you strike your foot against a stone. You will tread upon the lion and cobra, the young lion and the serpent you will trample down. Because he has loved Me, therefore I will deliver him; I will set him securely on high, because he has known My name. He will call upon Me, and I will answer him; I will be with him in trouble; I will rescue him, and honor him. With a long life I will satisfy him, and let him behold My salvation.

Mom grew up in a country church, with parents who loved her. As a teenager, she had a habit of slipping out to pray in her daddy's orange grove. One day Jesus so immersed her in His Spirit, she was forever changed. Having read of such experiences in the Bible (Acts 2), she knew it was of God. Her love for Jesus intensified, her prayer life increased, and her zeal embarrassed some people. Deacons from her church asked her not to return to their services. She was only sixteen. Today, wise leaders look for people who pray and are confident and fearless about Christ, regardless of their age or formal training.

My earliest childhood memory is of kneeling in prayer by Mom's bed. Generally, I was on one side of Mom, and my twin brother was on the other. Mom told us to talk to Jesus ourselves in our own words. She insisted we pray out loud, especially difficult to do with my brother listening.

We knelt and prayed in turn. I distinctly recall feeling God's presence in the room—it was so strong, the hair stood up on the back of my neck. I looked around in case I could actually see Him. **When Mom prayed, she talked to Jesus like He really was there.** I'm sure she knew her prayers were impacting us. When Mom prayed, things happened—we got to experience them firsthand.

My brother and I were only about five years old when we had to practice what Mom taught us. At that time, Dad was an alcoholic. He had been bitterly hurt during the Depression and lost many years to alcohol. He was one of the reasons Mom prayed so much.

Mom became severely ill with tuberculosis (TB) and was quarantined to a special sanitarium an hour from home. Although Dad took us to see her on the weekends, we weren't allowed in her room. The nurses rolled her in a wheelchair onto the upper deck so she could see us, and we stood on the grass below, waving to her, her image blurred by our tears. We could see her and call to her, but we couldn't hug her or climb up on her lap. We missed our momma.

Weeks passed. Grandma and other relatives came to our house to take care of us. One day I told my brother that we were going to pray until Jesus healed Momma. We shoved the piano bench against the living room wall, knelt down, and began to pray. We prayed hard and loud. We prayed and prayed and prayed. We got louder and louder. Eventually, the relatives couldn't take it any more and ran us outside, chasing us out of the house with a broom. Later, Grandma told Mom we prayed so hard the veins in our necks stood out.

The next day, something happened to Mom. Lying in her hospital bed, she had a vision of Jesus. Dressed in a white robe with long sleeves, He walked into her room in the tuberculosis sanitarium in Tampa, Florida. Calling her by name, He said, "Myrtle, when they take the x-ray pictures, it will be gone." With that, He leaned over and extended His hand into her body up to the cuff of His sleeve. When He withdrew His hand, He disappeared.

A few minutes later, as Mom lay there weeping and laughing, her doctor came in to announce they were going to take more x-rays. Mom said, "Go ahead, but it's gone." After viewing the new x-rays, the doctor told her, "We don't understand. We see the scar where the TB was, but it's gone." They released her after a few days of tests and observation. The TB never returned. Mom came home.

Mom reaped the "first fruits" of teaching her children to pray. **We used what she taught us in order to pray effectively for her!** She reaped long-term benefits, too. Of her five children, three of us are in ministry today. I pray daily and have taught my children how to pray. Mom's prayers have already impacted three generations of her family.

When I was a teenager, Mom started a "prayer chain" ministry. People called the church with prayer requests, which were then forwarded to Mom. She called five people to pray, and each of them called five more people. It usually wasn't long, sometimes only hours, when the phone rang again with news that the prayers had been answered, and the good news would be relayed back along the prayer chain. What an awesome experience, witnessing those prayers being answered so dramatically.

Read

Today, when I hurt or am in need, when I sin or grow spiritually cold, I pray. When I fight our spiritual enemy in warfare, when I stand in the gap for my family, when I intercede for the church, I pray. When I want fellowship with God, when my heart overflows with gratitude for His blessings, I pray.

There is no age requirement for prayer. Children can pray with powerful results. Teenagers can move Heaven. Gray-haired men and women can shape families' destinies. **The critical thing is that *somebody* prays effectively.** Discover, activate, and strengthen your purpose and dreams through targeted prayer. "The effective prayer of a righteous man can accomplish much" James 5:16.

Teach your children by praying with them. Learn to fight the good fight of faith. Get in the ring and start swinging. Learn by doing. When the devil comes knocking at the door to your family, tell him, "Over my dead body," get on your knees and PRAY. Keep at it until you get results. Take what you become in prayer and impart it to your children and to those who look to you. You never know where your journey in prayer will take you or what impact it will have. The important thing is to do it!

Mom's prayer chain didn't end when she died. Years ago, I joined my pastor and a visiting minister on a walk around the grounds of my home church. Pastor told the visitor that my mother had started a prayer chain that functioned for decades until the church relocated to this new property. At that time, the ministry expanded into 24-hours-a-day, 7-days-a-week prayer with intercessors praying from a 7-story prayer tower by the church.

> There is no age requirement for prayer.

A few years later, to commemorate a church anniversary, prayer cards were assembled representing answers to prayer from that prayer group. Thousands of answered prayers were recorded! What a testimony! What a conclusion to a teenage girl's prayers in an orange grove!

Scripture says if even one parent is a Christian believer, the children will be set apart to God (1 Corinthians 7:14). That happened to me. And the results continue today—I regularly pray in my home. My sons pray. Family and friends report answers to prayer as the awesome adventure continues. We can go now to what Jesus called the "secret place" or the "inner room." He said if we would pray in secret, our Father in Heaven would reward us publicly (Matthew 6:6).

Like the children who entered the large, wooden wardrobe in C.S. Lewis' Chronicles of Narnia books, we step into our inner room where time becomes inconsequential as we do exploits for the King. It is there that our kingly authority and abilities function, and our destiny is fulfilled.

> You never know where your journey in prayer will take you or what impact it might have. The important thing is to do it !

Who knows what our prayers will start or what the results will be? There is no limitation to prayer—we can go anywhere. We don't need to worry about our appearance, our education, our credentials—we can each go as we are.

**We are today what we became in prayer last year.
Let the adventure begin!**

Adventures in Prayer

RELATED SCRIPTURES:
Psalm 5:1-3
Proverbs 15:29
Matthew 21:22
Mark 9:29
Acts 12:1-7
Ephesians 6:18
Philippians 4:6
Colossians 4:2
James 5:13-18

APPLICATIONS:
If you knew God would hear and answer the next prayer you prayed, what would it be? What's stopping you from praying that prayer now?

How would you characterize your prayer relationship with God? Do you listen as well as speak? How can you improve your prayer life?

Why does God want people to pray?

What answers to prayer have you received?

What have you learned about prayer by listening to others pray? Have you ever sung next to someone and realized you could pick up the resonance from his voice to help you sing? Could praying with someone help you?

Keep a prayer journal of your requests and your impressions of how you ought to pray over them. Mark answers you receive to your prayers. Try something like this for each major prayer item you bring before God:

Date: (___/___/___)   Prayer Request:
                       Prayer Strategy:
                       Results:
Date: (___/___/___)   Prayer Answered:

Pray out loud with your children. Begin by thanking God for them. Encourage your children to pray by praying with them and letting them pray with you.

PRAYER:
Heavenly Father, You have drawn me into an adventure in prayer. By Your help, I gain victory over the things that hinder my relationship with You. Lord, I desire to see the results of my prayers, so teach me to pray effectively, to intercede with courage for my family, friends, church, business, and country. Allow me, Lord Jesus, the privilege of being changed by You in Your presence and becoming an encourager to those around me. Thank You, Lord. Amen.

2

"Though my father and mother forsake me, the Lord will receive me" Psalm 27:10.

[handwritten: Christianity is a close relationship with God. Sit on his lap - Feel his heart]

Your Father Loves You

[handwritten: IN WHAT WAYS DOES GOD SPEAK TO US? The WORD - SPIRIT. GODLY PEOPLE - CIRCUMSTANCES. THROUGH HIS CREATION]

Just as a true father relates to his children, our Father in Heaven bonds with us as we experience Him. One way we experience Him is through His voice. God speaks to us in many ways. The most familiar way is through His creation, where even the heavens declare His glory, handiwork, and righteousness (Psalms 19:1; 97:6). The next is through the Bible. As we read and study His words, the Holy Spirit applies them to us. God speaks through people, such as loving parents, anointed ministers, godly community leaders, and, sometimes, even our enemies. God speaks through circumstances. Since we never hear perfectly, God mercifully addresses us through His providential work behind the scenes. And after we are born again, God speaks to us personally, by the gentle voice of His Spirit in our inner man. "My sheep hear My voice, and I know them, and they follow Me" John 10:27. *[handwritten: Call cows]*

God is a Father. God enjoys fellowship with His children. He enjoyed fellowship with Adam in the Garden in the beginning and will enjoy fellowship with you and me today.

**Our Father in Heaven bonds
with us as we hear His voice.**

I had no trouble seeing a little bit of Heaven on earth growing up in Florida. I loved the woods, the trails, the tree forts, the crystal clear cold springs we swam in. I knew God was awesome to create such a place. I heard about God from my mother, our Sunday School teacher, and our pastor. I read the Gideon New Testament we received at school.

And there were Christian youth camps, the highlight of each great Florida summer. In my early teens, at one of these camps, I had quite an experience as I waited on God around the altar after evening meetings. Dozens of guys and girls met the Lord there, and many made commitments to Him. These kids weren't afraid to pray, to cry before God, and some waited on Him into the night hours, stretched out on the carpet between the altars at the front of the camp chapel.

I came home with an increased zeal for God and found myself devouring the Bible, reading it for hours at a time. Walking the trails near my home one day, I wrestled over a deeper commitment to God. It was dusk, near the end of my walk, when I realized my heart was settled. I said "Yes!" to God. Immediately, I began to speak words I had not planned to speak. I said, "I will preach the Gospel, I will fish for men, and I will walk in the power of Your Spirit." It seemed like the Holy Spirit was filling me up. I felt on fire and drunk at the same time. On this occasion, the voice of God came through me as I prophesied by the influence of the Holy Spirit.

I later learned that about half the time the Holy Spirit fell on people in the Book of Acts, they prophesied. That ratio should still be true today. Some churches have relegated the

Holy Spirit to past history. Others have made Him equivalent only to the gift of tongues. He is much more wonderful than that, and He is very close to us.

His voice is that of the most loving and powerful Father in the universe!

God spoke to me again in the countryside around my home. We lived far from town, near the phosphate mine where my father and neighbors worked. While out hiking with my dog, I read my New Testament. When I read His words, I felt the Holy Spirit's presence. I felt His love surround me. Mom had health problems, and Dad was an alcoholic. I needed heavenly reassurance. It was personal encouragement from my Heavenly Father, delivered to me through His Word by means of the Holy Spirit.

I have learned that when God speaks to us, we had better hold on to His message. He knows we will need it later on. Paul told Timothy, "In accordance with the prophecies previously made concerning you, that by them you may fight the good fight" 1 Timothy 1:18. We will need the prophetic word for the warfare to come. The Holy Spirit reveals the mind of Christ, thoughts from God, through revelatory gifts such as prophecy.

God spoke to me again during my freshman year of college. Entering the church sanctuary one evening, a godly woman, an intercessor who prayed a great deal for us young people, caught my sleeve and said God had shown her that Isaiah 54 was especially for me, that I would need it the rest of my life.

I discovered parts in that chapter that uniquely applied to someone growing up amidst the turmoil accompanying an alcoholic parent. "Fear not, for you will not be put to shame; neither feel humiliated, for you will not be disgraced; but you will forget the shame of your youth" Isaiah 54:4. Certainly there was much shame and no peace in my home. The rest of the chapter also encouraged me. "'My lovingkindness will not be removed from you, and My covenant of peace will not be shaken,' says the Lord who has compassion on you" Isaiah 54:10.

Over the years, other passages from this chapter about rejection and being "fiercely assailed" became real to me. My Heavenly Father's words to me from the Bible were true! They encouraged and sustained me.

Years later, God gave me a beautiful wife. When time came for our first child to be born, we were confronted with an emergency. Monitors indicated a problem with the baby's heartbeat. Watching from the doorway while the doctors and nurses huddled over my wife, I prayed, "God, remember Your covenant!" God kept His word. Our son was born, perfectly formed, in a nearly normal delivery.

> **When God speaks to us, it's because we need those words for the warfare to come!**

[handwritten notes: 1 COR 10:13 God will provide A WAY of escape]

[handwritten notes: PSALM 91 - DAVID's WRECK]

After our second son was born, I discovered "my" chapter proclaimed, "All your sons will be taught of the Lord; and the well-being of your sons will be great. In righteousness you will be established; you will be far from oppression, for you will not fear; and from terror, for it will not come near you" Isaiah 54:13, 14. I told my wife, "God let me know ten years ago that we would have boys!" Later, we had two more boys. God had spoken words that caused me to love and trust Him as I experienced Him.

God kept His word.

24

God spoke to Adam, His earthly creation. God came looking for him in the "cool of the day" Genesis 3:8. It was the time of day when the winds change. God will come calling us, too, when the winds around us change—crucial times when we face new beginnings, when we are about to encounter trials or when we enter a new season in our life.

Jesus heard His Father's audible voice on at least three occasions while He was on earth. One of the most notable was after He submitted Himself to John the Baptist to be baptized. Jesus heard His Father say, "This is My beloved Son, in whom I am well pleased" Matthew 3:17. As the pattern Son, Jesus was both the role model for our lives as well as the sacrifice for our sins. As the Son, Jesus lived for His Father's approval. This voice from Heaven came immediately before Jesus faced Satan in the wilderness.

If Jesus needed to hear His Father's voice, don't we need to hear it even more? Just like our children need to hear our words of love spoken over them, we need to hear loving words from our Heavenly Father. Sometimes God speaks, but we don't hear Him. Maybe we thought it was only thunder (John 12:29). Could He have already spoken words over you that you missed?

Jesus knew His Father's love and prayed that we would know the same love. "Thou didst send Me, and didst love them, even as Thou didst love Me" John 17:23. As Jesus prepared His disciples for His departure, He told them they could pray in His Name to the Father "for the Father Himself loves you" John 16:27. Jude said, "Keep yourselves in the love of God" Jude 1:21.

> Just like our children need to hear our words of love spoken over them, we need to hear loving words from our Heavenly Father.

Yes, we need to know the fear of the Lord. It is the beginning of wisdom, and it will cause us to come clean before God. But Jesus wants us to know that **the Father Himself loves us**. The most powerful Father in the universe has personal affection and concern for you and me. In the original text, the word for love in this passage is "phileo," the love of a friend. It is not a distant or universal love—it is personal and relational. It is possible because of Jesus!

**The most powerful Father in the universe has
personal affection for us.**

The Father loves us **before we are able** to return His love. "For while we were still **helpless** ... Christ died for the ungodly" Romans 5:6.

The Father loves us **before we are worthy.** "God demonstrates His own love toward us, in that while we were yet **sinners,** Christ died for us" Romans 5:8.

The Father loves us **while we still hate Him.** For while we were **enemies,** "we were reconciled to God through the death of His Son" Romans 5:10.

> The most powerful Father in the universe has personal affection and concern for you and me.

We all belong to at least one of these categories—helpless, sinners or enemies of God. Nevertheless, the Father Himself loves us and wants fellowship with us. We can come to the Father only through the sacrifice of Jesus on the cross. That's where all the evil we deserved was placed on Jesus so that all the righteousness He earned could be available to us. That's where Jesus demonstrated the depth and breadth of God's love for us.

**God will speak to us so that we can experience
His love and faithfulness.**

The shortest distance between you and God is faith!
Hearing God will increase your faith. "Faith comes from
hearing, and hearing by the word of Christ" Romans 10:17.
Put your faith in Christ now. Keep yourself in the love of
God. His love is for you. He will make up with His own love
what is missing in your heart. He will complete the unfinished
fathering. His love will enable you to persevere. He will speak
to you so that you can experience His love and faithfulness
first hand. Remember, **the Father Himself loves you!**

Your Father Loves You

RELATED SCRIPTURES:
Deuteronomy 30:19-20
Psalms 10:17, 18; 16:7
Isaiah 50:4
Isaiah 54
Luke 8:18
John 14:18, 21, 23, 26; 16:13-15, 26, 27
2 Corinthians 6:17, 18
Hebrews 3:7, 8, 19

APPLICATIONS:
Whom did God use to speak to you? Have you thanked them for their influence upon you? If you've lost touch with them, ask God to bless them wherever they are. Can God use you to speak His heart to someone? Who?

God is capable of arranging events in order to speak to you. What circumstances has God used to get your attention and redirect your life?

List Scriptures you consider to be personally "yours." How have they influenced your life? How can you cooperate with God's Word in your life?

If God were to speak to you out of His Word right now, what would He say to you? If you heard His voice, what do you think it would sound like?

Have you made any commitments to the Lord? It has been said, "Nothing you do for God will have its fullest meaning until you have told Him you will do anything." That involves a lot of trust. But it's only as you take small steps that you learn to walk. You have to trust Him with your fears to be able to trust Him at all. Have you trusted Him with your secret fears and sins—with all of your heart? He can handle it—He already knows it all anyway, and He has made provision for you by what Jesus accomplished on the cross.

Share with your family things God has told you or your parents which came to pass.

PRAYER:

Heavenly Father, thank You for loving me. I put my faith in Jesus Christ who saved me from my sins. I receive Jesus as my Savior and Lord of my life. Father, make up with Your love what is missing in my heart. Complete the unfinished fathering. I confess it is hard for me to trust. Speak to me so I can experience Your love and faithfulness first hand. Father, I commit myself to You and open my heart to You. Amen.

3

Hearing His voice is the
beginning of fatherhood.

Page 32 next page

Hearing Daddy's Voice

My wife Kay became more beautiful with a God-given glow every day her pregnancy progressed. As an expectant father, I was impressed with the ever-increasing reality of the coming event. I brought home special "morning sickness tolerant food," assembled nursery furniture, took child birthing classes—in other words, prepared to become a father. I also discovered I was talking to Kay's expanding abdomen, speaking to the child we did not yet know. I told the unborn baby that we loved him, and I prayed for mother and child, that both would be safe in the birthing process. I spoke blessings over the baby.

Four sons later, I believe those kids were blessed by my prayers and words even before their birth! In fact, I believe that a father's deeper voice resonates in the mother's womb! We have Scriptural evidence that an unborn baby is aware of voices around it—"When Elizabeth heard Mary's greeting, the baby leaped in her womb" Luke 1:41. Maybe it's a "guy" thing, but I advise dads to speak to their babies even before they are born, blessing them and prophesying, speaking "well words" over them of good things to come.

We all need to hear our daddy's voice speak positive, encouraging, motivational words to us. These lay a foundation in our inner man from which to face the issues of life. Jesus heard His Father's voice after He was baptized in water—His Father audibly spoke to Him from Heaven with affirming, encouraging words. "This is My beloved Son, in whom I am well-pleased" Matthew 3:17. Soon thereafter, Jesus resisted the devil's temptations in the wilderness by countering with what He heard from His Father. Quoting Deuteronomy 8:3, Jesus said, "Man shall not live on bread alone, but on every word that proceeds out of the mouth of God" Matthew 4:4.

We *live* by a "proceeding" word. We draw life itself, strength, endurance, faith, direction, and everything that sustains us by hearing our Father's voice. **Jesus equated fresh words from God with fresh bread to sustain our life.** I am not talking about new doctrine or additional Scriptures but rather God's voice made personal to us by the Holy Spirit. "But the helper, the Holy Spirit, whom the Father will send in My Name, He will teach you all things" John 14:26. Jesus often withdrew from people and ministry activity to spend time with His Father. "After He had sent the crowds away, He went up on the mountain by Himself to pray" Matthew 14:23. Jesus established a pattern for us to follow.

He who has ears let him hear

God is continually speaking; only our hearing is intermittent. He has a "proceeding" word, an ongoing, fresh word. He is a healthy Father. He is not sick or asleep or so distracted that He cannot spend time with us. Elijah taunted the prophets of Baal that perhaps their god was sleeping (1 Kings18:27). Many religious systems and denominations today assert that God is "asleep," that God no longer speaks to His people.

Cessationism is when people believe that God has ceased answering prayer, stopped being actively involved in our midst. This is simply not true. There is no logical ending to the Book of Acts—we are still living in the age of the Holy Spirit. He is alive and well on planet Earth, doing the stuff Jesus said He (the Holy Spirit) would do. "It is to your advantage ... when He, the Spirit of truth comes, He will guide you ... He will speak ... He will glorify me" John 16:7-14.

Hearing God is crucial: "If you have trouble hearing God speak, you are in trouble at the very heart of your Christian experience" (Henry T. Blackaby, *Experiencing God*, p. 36). God is ready, able, and willing to speak. In a healthy relationship, communication is necessary and natural in order to exchange information, express affection, mature, and accomplish things.

Childhood memories affect our response to life as adults. Do you remember the sound of your father coming home at the end of the day? Was it pleasant, or was it threatening or intimidating? The sound of your daddy's voice can have a powerful effect on you, creating a sense of well-being and anticipation or fear and insecurity.

I grew up in central Florida when miles of wilderness created fascinating situations. Dad and his friends gathered in the living room and talked late into the night after the rest of us went to bed. Their stories of deer poaching, black panthers stalking the campsite, fishing trips, and other stuff real men experienced were so irresistible, I'd crawl out from under my warm, comfortable blanket, sneak down the hall, and hide behind the couch. I wanted to listen; I especially loved hearing Dad's voice. Kids are easily drawn to a loving dad, desiring that special connection. For a long

> There is no logical ending to the Book of Acts—we are still living in the age of the Holy Spirit.

time, I treasured a worn, hand-written note that simply said, "Gone fishing—Dad." Children desperately need a healthy, loving dad, one who cares enough to take time with them—to talk with and listen to them. This relationship is important with our natural fathers—critical with our Heavenly Father.

We need to hear our Heavenly Father's voice. When was the last time you heard from God? Are you making yourself available? Are you cultivating your listening skills? Will you crawl out of your comfortable place and listen to His stories, stories that will change, motivate, and electrify your life?

Fatherhood and sonship are an integral part of our walk with God—"I will be a Father to you, and you shall be sons and daughters to Me" 2 Corinthians 6:18. When you grow in your relationship with Christ, you grow in relationship with your Heavenly Father. **What you missed as a child with your natural father is healed in your relationship with your Heavenly Father.** Intellectual assent and religious knowledge alone are inadequate. Personal knowledge of God results in intimacy that enables us to embrace Him as Father and mature as sons and daughters.

God acts like a daddy toward us: "Then I raised up some of your sons to be prophets and some of your young men to be Nazirites" (young men or women with especially dedicated lifestyles) Amos 2:11. God calls our offspring, and He prepares their personality and experiences for the tasks He appoints for them. God is personally involved with us and our offspring. He behaves toward us in every way as a father. "And you have forgotten the exhortation which is addressed to you as sons, 'My son, do not regard lightly the discipline of the Lord, nor faint when you are reproved by Him; for those whom the Lord loves He disciplines' ... shall we not rather be subject to the Father of spirits and live?" Hebrews 12:5, 6, 9.

God is a loving Father who disciplines and trains His own children. Routinely hearing our father, seeking his advice and love, prepares us to establish a pattern of seeking, hearing, and receiving from our Heavenly Father. "Upon You I was cast from birth; You have been my God from my mother's womb" Psalm 22:10.

When we first experience God and are born again, we are "newborn sons." "The Spirit Himself testifies with our spirit that we are children of God" Romans 8:16. The Greek word for children here is "tekna," "newborn sons," in the sense of being direct offspring.

We receive an impartation from God that changes us and makes us become like Him. "You have received a spirit of adoption as sons by which we cry out, 'Abba! Father!'" Romans 8:15. The original text here, "pneuma uiothesias," means "spirit of adoption as sons" or "spirit of sonship."

After we have walked with God and have begun to recognize His voice, our sonship grows, and we become "maturing sons." "For all who are being led by the Spirit of God, these are sons of God" Romans 8:14. The word for sons here is "uioi," "maturing sons," in the sense of learning and hearing, manifesting the character and destiny of the one we are following. The spirit we receive leads us into maturity, into an ability to hear our Father's voice. Growing in maturity requires recognizing and following God's voice.

The voice of God is that of the most loving and powerful Father in the universe! There is no mistaking His sound! It's not religious or sectarian. It's not controlling or critical. It's redemptive, patient, loving, constructive, encouraging, longsuffering—everything you ever wanted in a Father—and more. It is also powerful!

Even if you never had a natural father love you, you can experience your Heavenly Father's love. "Although my father and my mother have forsaken me, yet the Lord will take me up [adopt me as His child]" Psalm 27:10 AMP.

God is a faithful Father. This became real to me in my early teens. I frequently walked alone and prayed in the woods near my home. In my back pocket, I carried the New Testament and Psalms the Gideons gave me in third grade. On the trail one day, as I read this passage, the Holy Spirit wrapped me in His love. I felt God's assurance that He was with me, no matter what happened, and He would fulfill that Scripture in my life. The power of this encounter with God impacted my life then and continues even now.

Why don't you let Him speak to you through your Bible today? Make it your habit to read His Word so His Spirit can make application in your life. Do you want to hear your Daddy's voice? Do you need His words of encouragement and direction? Have you received all the fathering you need? Have you become all the father your children desire?

Call on God now. He has things to say to you. If it's been a while since you heard the sound of a real Father, start listening for His voice today.

The starting point of real fatherhood is hearing your Heavenly Father's voice. Listen to His words, His impressions, the witness of the Holy Spirit to you of His Fatherhood and your adoption into His family. Let's do what Jesus did—listen for our Father's voice so we can do what He says.

Hearing Daddy's Voice

RELATED SCRIPTURES:
Genesis 3:8
Genesis 5:22-24; Jude 14
Deuteronomy 28
Matthew 3:16, 17; Mark 9:7; John 12:28
Matthew 4:4; 7:24

APPLICATIONS:
"Therefore take care how you listen; for whoever has, to him shall more be given; and whoever does not have, even what he thinks he has shall be taken away from him" Luke 8:18. How you listen determines what you have. Do you "have your ears on"? How do you know?

How do you think Adam's heart responded at the sound of God's voice when they met in the garden?

After he became a father, Enoch enjoyed fellowship with God for hundreds of years. Enoch, seventh from Adam, was the first prophet mentioned in the Bible (Genesis 5:21-24; Jude 14). Do you think Enoch's walks with God contributed to his prophetic anointing? What happens when you are in God's presence? Do you think Enoch became a little bit more like God as a result of hearing His voice?

Jesus heard His Father audibly speak to Him at least three times. Why do you think Jesus needed to hear His Father's voice? How did the words the Father spoke to Jesus reveal the Father's purpose?

Read Deuteronomy 8:3 and find where and when Jesus used this passage of Scripture. *Man does not live by bread alone but by every word that comes from the mouth of the Lord* Why is it important to pay attention when God speaks to you? What happens if you do not listen?

What does it mean to build on a solid foundation? What is your life built on? How do you discover the foundations for your life?

Name Bible characters who demonstrate the keys of hearing and obeying in order to receive blessings.

PRAYER:
Heavenly Father, Your Word resonates in my heart. My mind can barely comprehend what I feel in my heart as I listen to You. All of Your actions toward me have been to redeem me and bring me into Your family. Thank You for giving Your Son for me. Thank You for giving me a hearing heart to walk with You. Jesus is my Lord and Savior, and You are my Heavenly Father from now on. Amen.

4

*A fresh vision from God will
change your circumstances.*

HABAKKUK 2:4
WRITE THE VISION DOWN

Embrace Your Vision

Our Heavenly Father is a communicating God. Jesus spoke what was in His Father's heart. "I speak these things as the Father taught Me ... I always do the things that are pleasing to Him ... I speak the things which I have seen with My Father" John 8:28, 29, 38. When Jesus spoke for God, He spoke the same way the Father spoke. Jesus prophesied because God is prophetic. **God has a history of revealing things.**

God's activities begin with a word. The language of the Holy Spirit is frequently expressed through dreams and visions. When the word comes, it may be in a dream or a picture, not just in a "thus sayeth the Lord." Jacob had such a dream encounter, a word from God in picture form that revealed God's activity in his life.

Jacob was in a business relationship with his father-in-law, Laban, easily a prototype of the struggles many believers encounter when they attempt a joint Christian business enterprise. Perhaps you

> God's
> activities
> begin with a
> word.

identify with Jacob when he said that Laban "has cheated me and changed my wages ten times" Genesis 31:7.

Jacob had a dream (Genesis 31:10) that gave him a strategy to deal with the imbalanced family relationship. As his new wages, he would accept only striped or speckled animals from the flocks. Acting on his dream, Jacob placed striped sticks in front of the healthy flocks at the watering troughs and removed the sticks when sickly flocks approached to drink. The flocks mated and conceived at the watering troughs, and the healthy sheep had speckled and striped lambs. These striped and speckled animals were Jacob's new wages, negotiated according to the dream's directives.

Jacob's flocks grew and prospered, more than making up for his prior losses. In the natural, there was no reason for striped sticks to affect the genetic process of the mating sheep or goats. In the spirit, however, Jacob was being taught the importance of vision and of acting on your vision.

Vision precedes fruitfulness. The dreams we carry can be birthed in our life. We need to pray for a "God-given" vision. **We are today what we became in prayer last year.** The present circumstances of our life and family don't have to be the finale. **A fresh vision from God, if acted upon, will change our circumstances,** but we don't want just any dream—we want God's dream.

> The present circumstances of our life and family don't have to be the finale.

Jacob was shown that conception would take place at the watering trough. Water is symbolic of the Spirit. Vision plus water equals conception. A divine vision waits for a divine outpouring of the water of the Spirit. The vision is the seed, but germination requires water.

Singles, do you envision a mate? Couples, do you dream for fruitfulness and blessing in your family? God can impart a dream for wholeness, increase, and joy in your home.

In Scripture, pictures of healthy family relationships are seen in Proverbs, the Song of Solomon, and Ephesians. They are modeled by the Father's relationship with Jesus and Jesus' relationship with the church. God can plant a vision of wholeness in your marriage. He can give you dreams for your children and grandchildren.

WHAT IS SEEN IN OUR LIVES GETS INTO OUR DESCENDANTS

Sometimes a natural picture can help. Perhaps this is why Scripture teaches us to "model the message" for the next generation. "Be imitators of me, just as I also am of Christ" 1 Corinthians 11:1. What is seen in our lives gets into our descendants' or disciples' spirits where they carry it until it is also birthed in their lives. "The things you have learned and received and heard and seen in me, practice these things" Philippians 4:9.

We must be full of the Word of God and learn to rest in His presence. Then, at the right time, the anointing will come, conception will take place in the realm of the Spirit, and we will begin to see in the natural what God showed us in the spirit.

My wife Kay and I have four sons. We taught an adult Sunday School class comprised of couples, singles, and some newlyweds. They were around our family a lot as we opened our home for hospitality and prayer times, and the boys joined us in class. We noticed something remarkable with these couples. Over a 6-year span, all who became pregnant had boys. It is interesting to speculate that what these couples observed in our family in the presence of the Spirit of God was birthed in the natural. Like the striped sticks, what these couples saw is what they got! In the presence of God, they had a vision—BOYS!

In another church years earlier, the elders chose Mother's Day to publicly pray for several barren couples who desired to have children. My wife and I always sat close to the front, and the "overflow" that day hit us as we witnessed the prayer for fruitfulness in those marriages. Not only did Kay become pregnant, but in that church of 200 couples, forty babies were born the next year! The week Kay gave birth to our fourth son, four other ladies from church had babies at the same hospital. The elders' prayer was spiritually powerful, and the natural results were dramatic.

God called Abram and promised him a family; however, Abram and Sarai were barren. One night, God spoke to Abram in a vision, saying, "Do not fear, Abram, I am a shield to you; your reward shall be very great" Genesis 15:1. At this, Abram began to question God, since Sarai was still barren. Then God instructed Abram to go outside and look up. "Now look toward the heavens, and count the stars, if you are able to count them ... So shall your descendants be" Genesis 15:5.

God used something in the natural that was so plentiful as to be uncountable to impart a vision of fruitfulness to Abram's mind. God had to stretch his understanding. Abram obediently grasped what God was showing him. "Then he believed in the Lord, and He reckoned it to him as righteousness" Genesis 15:6. You, too, must mix faith with the word you receive from God.

The vision stuck with Abram, who became Abraham, "father of a multitude," and the believing of it was righteousness to Abraham. We are the fruit of his vision. And truly, it is impossible to count the natural descendants as well as the spiritual descendants of Abraham—just as God told him it would be.

Do we carry God's vision or our own vision for our life? God has a personal vision for each of us. **Holding that vision, let's wait in His presence.** There, where the water of the Spirit quenches the thirst of our soul, our Heavenly Father will cause conception and eventual birthing to occur. Vision plus Spirit equals conception. In God's presence, dreams come true!

Let's embrace our God-given vision and wait in His presence so that we can "do the stuff!"

Embrace Your Vision

RELATED SCRIPTURES:
Job 33:13-18
Proverbs 29:18
Daniel 2:19
Matthew 1:20; 2:12, 13, 19, 22
Luke 24:49
John 14:26
Acts 2:17; 9:10-12; 10:3, 17, 19; 16:9; 18:9

APPLICATIONS:
After reading the related Scriptures above, do you believe God can lead by dreams and visions?

Has God imparted dreams and visions to you?

How do you know which ones are from Him?

Have you acted on them? Why or why not?

Are you the same person you were a year ago? How have God's words to you changed you?

There are sometimes delays between prayers and answers. What keeps you going when there is a delay?

Do you see a correlation between the Holy Spirit's activity and an increase of dreams and visions? Explain.

PRAYER:

Heavenly Father, I desire a "God-given" vision; I want Your best. My present circumstances are not the finale. Impart to me Your dream for my wholeness and for joy in my home (church, business, community). Stretch my understanding. Fill me with Your Word and let me rest in Your presence. Teach me to pray the kinds of prayers that bring Your dreams to pass. In Jesus' Name, I pray. Amen.

5

*Let's determine to empower
and release those around us.*

we had a class at work on empowerment.

The power of empowerment -
I would go to the Boss with an idea to
improve the workplace. Solve a problem.

Empower and Release

D avid was a man after God's own heart. He empowered
Solomon by laying up resources for him. Just as
farmers start with seed, so the generation after us
must start with "seed"—money and resources set aside for
them. A foolish person eats all the seed and leaves nothing to
sow for the following year's harvest. Resources must be left
for the next generation. "A good man leaves an inheritance
to his children's children" [third generation] Proverbs 13:22.
We should endeavor to be good men!

Good **Real men empower and release the next generation.**
"Empower" means to furnish the necessary tools, resources,
and knowledge and to encourage stamina, confidence,
endurance, and self-reliance so the next generation arrives
at its destiny prepared. "Release" means to enable the next
generation to step into its areas of responsibility clean, with
no strings attached that restrict, control, intimidate, or
otherwise entangle.

Abraham and Lot realized they had to separate because
the land they shared could no longer sustain their great
possessions. Abraham did not give Lot second best. He did

not send Lot to a faraway land in order to protect his own pastures. Instead, Abraham allowed Lot to choose first. "Is not the whole land before you? Please separate from me: if to the left, then I will go to the right; or if to the right, then I will go to the left" Genesis 13:9.

What kind of leader today would do that—give away part of the church membership, his top client list, the best sales territory? The general tendency is to preserve what's ours and send the associate minister, assistant manager, or junior member away—usually empty handed.

Fathers and leaders empower and release by investing themselves in the success of their offspring—even to the third generation. Christian ministers do this by burying their ministry in the Body of Christ, investing themselves in the success of the next generation of elders. Business leaders do this by mentoring those who are moving up in the company. Government leaders do this by serving to achieve the freedom of the governed.

My wife & Her Brother Whats 10,000 @ 21

IChron 22:

> **Fathers and leaders empower and release by investing themselves in the success of their offspring— even to the third generation.**

One way we empower those who follow us is by setting aside natural resources—money, property, tools. We don't spend or use it all on ourselves, seriously handicapping their beginnings. David left ample resources for Solomon to build the temple; he gathered supplies of iron, bronze, and timber. In addition, he gathered much gold and silver, to which Solomon added even more (1 Chronicles 22:3, 4, 14). He gave Solomon a foundation upon which to build, modeling the message of giving and increase.

1 CRon 28:11, & 19-20 Page 621

Another way to empower the next generation is by **imparting knowledge.** We teach them what we know that works. We give them the principles, the basics, a vision of goals, and an understanding of strategies. David left Solomon the plans for the temple (1 Chronicles 28:11, 19). How marvelous of God to impart a vision for His house to David so he could write it down for Solomon to grasp and implement! We, too, need to make the vision memorable and clear for the next generation.

Also, **we give those following us our commitment to their success.** This is our blessing, our affirmation, our encouragement, our endorsement. Every entrepreneur needs a sense of being "blessed." David told Solomon, "Be strong and courageous, and act; do not fear nor be dismayed, for the Lord God, my God, is with you" 1 Chronicles 28:20. Solomon felt David's commissioning, his purposeful commitment, imparted in a timely manner.

Control, fear, and passivity hinder our ability to empower and release. **Failing to bless is tantamount to imparting a curse.** How many children leave home without their parents' blessing or a portion of their resources because the parents think kids should have to tough it out on their own? How many young people called into ministry are resisted and criticized instead of supported and authorized by Christian elders? How many new businessmen have to "reinvent the wheel" because no senior manager mentors them? How many innovative, enthusiastic officials are hindered from implementing positive changes by "good ole' boy" politicians who've grown complacent and possessive of their position? Yielding some authority, or actually moving out of the way, can free

> Control, fear, and passivity hinder our ability to empower and release.

those with energy, creativity, and timely, new perspective to accomplish what past and current leaders have been unable or unwilling to do.

Jesus was both empowered and released by His Father. When He came up from the waters of baptism, His Father spoke from Heaven, "This is My beloved Son, in whom I am well pleased" Matthew 3:17. Those affirming words encouraged Jesus and prepared Him for the upcoming conflicts with the devil and the religious rulers. The Holy Spirit descended on Jesus to empower Him. Later, Scripture records the Father again establishing and endorsing Jesus' ministry. "This is My beloved Son, with whom I am well pleased; listen to Him!" Matthew 17:5. Then, a third time, His Father audibly encouraged Him, before Jesus went to the cross (John 12:28-29).

In many ways, we can affirm and equip those who come after us. Like the Father did with Jesus, parents can, in measure, impart blessing to their sons and daughters. This applies to church, business, and government leaders as well. **By our words and actions, we may continually impart encouragement, resources, and opportunities to the associates, assistants, and juniors in our arenas of leadership.**

> After preparing them for three years, Jesus entrusted His disciples to the Holy Spirit.

The final work is always done by God Himself. Since all authority in Heaven and on earth comes from God, the final benediction must be God's. Likewise, the final preparation and provision must be from God. After we have done all we can to fulfill our stewardship mandate to bless the next generation, we prayerfully present them to God for His finishing work.

After preparing them for three years, Jesus entrusted His disciples to the Holy Spirit. The Holy Spirit finished the work in them. He will finish it in you, too! And He will finish it in the sons and daughters you release to His care.

In every arena of responsibility, **let's empower and release those around us.** May we receive God's impartation of the Spirit of Fatherhood. Let's speak words of blessing, long life, health, and prosperity. Let's lay our hands on them and bless them. Let's not wait. Let's rise up, **overcome our own sense of inadequacy,** and bless our households, churches, businesses, and offices! A new sense of excitement and faith will emerge!

Every day, let's get beyond our insecurities, legalism, and fear of losing control. Let's determine to empower and release the next generation.

Empower and Release

RELATED SCRIPTURES:
Genesis 50:15-21
Matthew 20:25-28
1 Timothy 1:2, 18; 4:14; 6:20, 21
2 Timothy 1:2-7, 13, 14; 2:2

APPLICATIONS:
Are you restricted or controlled by things from the past? If yes, describe them and their lingering effects on you.

Are people and situations currently controlling or draining you? How do you move toward freedom in such a way that God can use these same situations to bless and promote you?

Do you restrict, control, or deliberately intimidate people? Have you kept yourself in an elevated position to make them aware of how much authority you have over them? How do you release them?

Should a husband control his wife? How about parents and children? Is it possible to govern without "over control"?

What resources can you share with the next generation or with those who look to you in your place of work or ministry? (time, money, materials, equipment, land, vehicles, knowledge, wisdom)

How could your actions at this point become a vital part of God's plan for His Kingdom?

How does God multiply His family?

PRAYER:
Heavenly Father, please forgive me for being controlling, fearful, or passive. Impart to me the Spirit of Fatherhood. By my words and actions, may I continually impart encouragement, resources, and opportunities to those who look to me. I determine, with Your help, to fulfill my stewardship mandate to empower, release, and bless the next generation. I thank You, Lord, in Jesus' Name. Amen.

PART TWO

BREAKING FREE TO
EFFECTIVENESS

6

Go to AN encounter for men.

Matthew 5:44 1450
Luke 6:32-38 (1550)
Romans 12:14-18
Have you forgiven everyone in your past?

> My freedom started when
> I tore up the IOU I held
> against Dad.

Tear Up the IOU

Talks about his dad being mean and abusive and lost but he was saved at 80 and became kind and gentle

Many of us bear the wounds of incomplete fathering. Even though called into ministry and functioning in it to a degree, I carried my own personal battles. One was very intense.

My dad was an alcoholic during my childhood, and I harbored deep resentment toward him. I couldn't bring friends home because I never knew what condition he'd be in. My earliest memories were of his drunkenness and violent temper. An out-of-control father is a terrifying, humiliating thing to a child. Because of what I felt toward my dad, I grew up with a sense of shame regarding my family.

In my early 20s, God dealt with me to forgive my parents for their flaws. He spoke to me especially about forgiving Dad for the bitter memories; however, the depth of my pain made forgiving him nearly impossible. I said the words, but the hurt, anger, and bitterness returned just as strong.

A message by the late interdenominational Bible teacher Derek Prince helped me understand the power of forgiveness. I thought I had to **feel like forgiving** my dad, but I learned that

forgiveness was a decision, that feelings would come later. The phrase "forgive our debts" in "The Lord's Prayer" directed me how to proceed. God had canceled the debts we owed Him, and He required us to do the same with the debts others owed us.

I wrote out a list of what my dad owed me: time together, hugs, words of affirmation, happy memories, an honorable father figure, a sense of self-worth. I couldn't remember one time that Dad put his hand on my shoulder or hugged me or told me he loved me. Dad owed me a lot. After I made the list, I verbally expressed my decision to forgive him. Then I tore up the IOU. **I literally shredded the paper.** My dad did not owe me anything anymore. **I had canceled the note.**

That act of forgiveness was a turning point in my life. **There were areas of emotional growth that I would never have passed through had I not made the decision to forgive.** I wrote him a letter, telling him I'd forgiven him for the hurts I'd experienced, that I'd done it in obedience to God, who had convicted me of harboring resentment. Eventually, I was able to tell Dad to his face that I had forgiven him. When I did, we were sitting at the kitchen table, my open Bible between us. He was quiet for a moment, then pointed to the Bible and said, "Son, keep doing what that Book says." Perhaps that played a role in what happened after Mom's death, several years later.

> I learned that forgiveness was a decision, that feelings would come later.

I had moved to another state, married, and started my own family. Mom died a week after our first child was born, and by then, Dad had retired. Before too long, a series of small strokes left him partially incapacitated and confined to a nursing home. Because of the strokes, he became even more hot-tempered and verbally abusive, so the staff was forced to sedate him. Over the years, when I visited him, he was usually too doped up to communicate. Mom had prayed for Dad's salvation for many years. So had I, yet it seemed Dad was beyond reach. But God had a plan.

We had moved back to my hometown, Lakeland, Florida. It was about ten years after Mom's death, and Dad was still in the nursing home, almost 80 years old. One Sunday afternoon, a nurse called to say Dad had fallen and broken his hip, and she needed me to sign the surgical release. A friend accompanied me to the hospital. We learned that, in preparation for the surgery, Dad's medication had been discontinued. When we walked into his room, I immediately saw that he was clear-headed.

I said, "Dad, I'm here to talk to you about the surgery and about Jesus." He said, "OK." I explained what had to be done, and he acknowledged the procedure and granted permission for the surgery. Then I reminded him how Mom had preached to him over the years about Jesus and how she had prayed for him to come to the Lord. Again, he acknowledged that was the case.

When I said, "Dad, I want to pray with you," tears rolled down his face. I asked him, "Do you know that the only way God could be just and also justify those who believe was to put our sins on Jesus?" Dad answered, "Yes," so I said, "Let's pray!" I led my dad in a prayer of repentance and a confession of faith. He didn't merely repeat my words; he prayed his own words, saying, "Lord, You are **my** Lord." Finally, I asked Dad to pray for me and bless me. He was hesitant at first, but then he laid his hand on me and prayed a beautiful blessing over my life. When we left, I hugged him. We were both crying. He said, "Son, I love you." All of this happened in just a few minutes. I looked at my friend, kneeling in the middle of the hospital room doorway, awestruck by the events God had orchestrated and allowed us to participate in.

Mom's 35 years of prayer had not failed! My friend witnessed the whole thing. Dad came to God, prayed a personal prayer, and prayed the first blessing over me in my whole life! We left the hospital room with a sense of incredible gratitude for what God had done.

When I'd first entered the hospital wing, the head nurse had commented on Dad's stubborn, abrasive manner with the nurses. The day after Dad prayed, I talked with the same nurse, asking if Dad would be put back on sedatives. She replied that he seemed different since the previous day, and she saw no reason for him to be sedated. That was the case, and Dad's change lasted. In the few years he had remaining, though he was very feeble, his tenderness toward God was evident. Every time I visited, I told him that I loved him, and he said that he loved me. God was faithful to answer our prayers for Dad.

Unfortunately, like most people, instead of taking positive action, I had first tried to blame someone else for my resentment and shame. There is a difference between acknowledging the cause of our hurt and blaming someone else for our reaction to it. Blaming others is a negative action that does not bring resolution to the pain. **Forgiveness is a positive action that changes us.** Just as God forgave us, we can forgive and release others.

> There is a difference between acknowledging the cause of our hurt and blaming someone else for our reaction to it.

Those most likely to hurt us are those closest to us—parents, spouse, friends, or pastor. We need to extend forgiveness to them even more than they need to receive it. A parent or friend can be long gone and still cause us pain if we harbor resentment. Our bitterness no longer hurts them—it now hurts only us. In fact, left untreated, it has the potential to completely destroy our life. In order to receive our own healing and liberty, we must release to God's judgment those who have hurt, disappointed, or betrayed us.

It's amazing how, the older I get, the more good memories I have of Dad. They had been buried under layers of pain. My memories became more complete—Dad was a good provider, hard worker, self-taught inventor, and poet, and he refused to give up, even in hard times. I have become more whole. The grace I extended to him has enabled me to receive more grace for myself. Jesus made it possible.

I didn't have to wait on a feeling. Forgiveness is a decision of the will. Emotions will follow a positive proclamation of the will. Make that decision. It may help to write out a list and literally tear up the IOU.

I now have four sons. Each will have to deal with his own list of my failures in order to mature and move on with God. But **I know I would not be where I am today had I not torn up the IOU I held against Dad.** Since then, I've followed the same principle in other situations with equally liberating results. Jesus paid my debt; I can cancel the debts owed me. Freely we have received—let's freely forgive.

When Dad died several years ago, my twin brother and I preached his funeral. The power of forgiveness was demonstrated by the testimony of the change in Dad and God's faithfulness to answer Mom's prayers. God is faithful. He will hear a wife's prayers. He will hear a little boy's prayers. He will hear your prayers. Nothing is impossible with God!

> Jesus paid my debt; I can cancel the debts owed me.

Go to AN oNCOUNTER - get iN TOUCH WITH ISSUES You MAY NOT REALIZE you Have

Tear Up the IOU

RELATED SCRIPTURES:
Psalm 94
Matthew 5:44-45
Luke 6:37, 38
Romans 12:14

APPLICATIONS:
Are you blaming someone? Do you believe you are "damaged goods"? Do you see yourself as a victim? Are you bitter or resentful?

What is God's remedy for those deeply-rooted, bitter feelings?

Is God dealing with you to forgive certain people? When you are quiet before God, the memory of them will come to you.

No defense of our rights is worth the separation from God it causes. What can you do now to begin the healing process, to allow the great Judge of the universe to take over your case?

Explain "Leave room for the wrath of God" Romans 12:19.

Next Page

Make a list of IOUs for major offenses, lifelong hurts, broken promises, betrayals, and abuse. Write down what the people owe you. Name names and acknowledge the cause of your pain. You can't forgive if you deny the reality or the source of the pain. Take responsibility for your own actions from this point forward by repenting for your reactions to the hurt and praying, "Lord, I forgive _____ for _____. I release him (her or them) from my judgment. I bless him by turning him over to You." Then tear up the lists, even dig a hole and "bury the remains." You're owed nothing— you have cancelled the debt. You've defeated it; it no longer affects you. If the feelings of bitterness temporarily return, remind yourself of your decision, and your emotions will line up with the choice of your will. It's gone because you decided to forgive, to let it go. You may not, and possibly should not, be in relationship with that person or group again, but you can experience God's grace for yourself, and you have put them in God's capable hands.

If there was sexual abuse or abuse of power by someone who is in a position to repeat the offense, get counsel from outside your immediate circle to reinforce your decision and for your protection and the protection of others.

PRAYER:
Heavenly Father, thank You for forgiving me. Thank You, Jesus, for canceling my debt. Reveal the hidden areas of bitterness, resentment, anger, and hatred in my heart, and deliver me from them as I act on my decision to willingly offer to my enemies the forgiveness I have freely received from You. Release these people and our families from the curse of my unforgiveness. Release me from the prison of resentment. Lord, You are faithful. With You all things are possible! Amen.

7

*Break the cycle of judgment
on successive generations.*

Imprisoned for Grandpa's Sins

1 Peter 1:18-19 P1889

A ll of us have a <u>history</u>. There were some ancestors in our family that Dad didn't want to talk about. Usually, most of our relatives are basically normal, but some exhibit a pattern of behavior that negatively affects us. Sometimes we get impacted big-time. That's what happened to a teenager named Daniel.

Daniel 9:2-19 PAGE 1313

Daniel prayed. He prayed a lot. The ninth chapter of Daniel is an intense prayer by a true statesman seeking the deliverance of his people. Daniel was possibly over eighty years old since the Babylonian captivity was 70 years in duration, and he was a teenager when captured. Along with other handsome, intelligent Hebrew youths, he was taken to Babylon. Tradition says he was immediately made a eunuch, and he served in the Babylonian courts after being properly trained.

*DANIEL PRAYED 70 YEARS AFTER HIS People Summed
Against God*

Seventy years later, Daniel had risen to be a statesman in Babylon. He faithfully prayed and read Scripture, discovering from the prophets' writings that the captivity could almost be over. He immediately set himself to pray and fast in order to see God's Word fulfilled. In that situation, some of us would have taken a "wait-and-see" approach—"Since God said it, let God do it." But Daniel **prayed** that it would happen since the time was evidently right. When finding a promise from God in the Scriptures, it is always appropriate to pray for its fulfillment rather than to just passively wait for it. **It is important that the subject of our prayer be firmly rooted in Scripture.** Daniel had his promise, and he sensed it was about to happen.

Daniel prepared to pray by humbling himself. He fasted to weaken himself and focus on God who was his strength, devoting his attention to special prayer for a season. This was not a routine prayer. He didn't get words from a prayer book. God led him in his preparation and words. It is important to come before God with clean hands and a pure heart when interceding for others. In light of the seriousness of the situation, **Daniel prayed a strategic prayer**, interceding for his entire nation. It was a strategic prayer because of its long-range implications. Furthermore, it was effective, ultimately causing God to dispatch the angel Gabriel, God's senior messenger, with vital information for Daniel.

Daniel realized there were conditions—repentance was required; however, the people who had sinned were dead. It was the second, third, and perhaps even the fourth generation after them who bore the consequences of their sins—"the curse has been poured out on us ... because of our sins and the iniquities of our fathers, Jerusalem and Thy people have become a reproach to all those around us" Daniel 9:11. Daniel was motivated for change. He had endured seventy years of captivity as the very real consequence of the sins of past leaders. Our captivity might not be as

> It is important that the subject of our prayer be firmly rooted in Scripture.

readily apparent as theirs, but the consequences of sin flow forward through time to us, too.

Most of the time, the discomfort of our present circumstances is a consequence of our own failure. Usually our personal failure brings localized pain, and we are aware of our misbehavior. But sometimes, the dilemma we are in is the result of moral failures by relatives or associates, and it's more difficult to identify the cause of our lingering hardship. Our dilemmas can be caused by personal or corporate decisions—sins of our nation, as well as personal sins.

When Daniel began to pray, he **rehearsed God's faithfulness,** proclaiming God's covenant-keeping nature. This is a good way for any of us to begin a prayer session—"I prayed to the Lord my God and confessed ... 'the great and awesome God, who keeps His covenant and lovingkindness for those who love Him'" Daniel 9:4. We need to remind ourselves of the bigness of God and the awesomeness of His power. We can rehearse, for the sake of our own faith, the many times God has heard and answered us. We should remember His covenant—sealed with the blood of Jesus—His guarantee of our privilege of approaching Him in prayer.

Daniel recited the transgressions and called it sin. Daniel named the sins—"We have sinned, committed iniquity, acted wickedly, and rebelled, even turning aside from Thy commandments and ordinances. Moreover, we have not listened to Thy servants the prophets, who spoke in Thy name to our kings, our princes, our fathers, and the people of the land" Daniel 9:5.

Then Daniel "named names." He said, "We have sinned ... our kings, our princes, and our fathers ... all Israel has transgressed Thy law." Do we have sins in our lineage or in our associations? Would we be willing to name the sin and the sinners? Some of us have ancestors who worshipped idols, sprinkling blood on skulls or stones to appease demons. Some have ancestors who harbored more subtle lawlessness—abuse of power, covetousness, racial hatred, sexual promiscuity, or religious pride.

Daniel named the leaders who had sinned. He stood before God and named names. When a pastor or official abuses authority, commits immorality, or mishandles finances, his behavior should not be excused. It's not merely a "personality quirk" or a reaction to stress. **When a parent or government leader abuses power, money, privilege, or intimacy, it is sin.** Legalism, sectarianism, or racism by parents, pastors, business leaders, or government officials is still sin, regardless of position or title. Parents or leaders do not sin without consequences. We cannot intercede for someone, or even forgive him, until we acknowledge his sin against us.

Daniel was courageous in his prayer. Going further, he stepped into the arena with the sinners, **changing from prosecutor to intercessor.** He said, **"We have sinned"** Daniel 9:5. This subtle but powerful change, Daniel's use of the personal pronoun "we," caused God to send the archangel Gabriel to him with instructions and assurances that the answer was on the way. **Our posture in prayer can result in angelic intervention in our circumstances.**

We cannot just blame our present circumstances on our ancestors. Doing so may be an accurate assessment, but it may not productively bring God's resources to bear in order to remedy the situation. Neither can we gloss over our forbears' failures. For instance, our fathers created a massive federal deficit equivalent to tens of thousands of dollars of debt for each U.S. family. We should rightly blame our fathers and leaders, but then we should repent with a determined attitude to take action. In this case, we should pray, vote, and ask God for supernatural wisdom and mercy to grow the economy to eliminate the debt.

Perhaps we had a drug-addicted or an alcoholic parent who sinned against us by depriving us of a stable, loving home life. It is important that we call it sin, but we don't stop there. We identify and repent for the consequences in us of that sin—hopelessness, dependency, passivity, depression, poverty, resentment—and look to God to intervene.

Similarly, perhaps our natural father deserted us or was a workaholic, an "absentee father." His absence created unmet needs and smoldering resentment. Where we were wounded, sin was at work, affecting the next generation, causing us to personally feel the consequences of the "sins of the fathers." Name names, call sin "sin," repent for its consequences, and ask God for mercy.

To the extent we feel "victimized" by our circumstances, we will be incapable of realizing our full potential. We must take responsibility to stand in the gap for our parents' and leaders' sins. **We must break the cycle of judgment by repenting and calling on God to intervene and vindicate us.**

Daniel had to wait 70 years to undo the consequences of his parents' sin, but **you and I can pray today.** In Jesus, "now is the day of salvation" 2 Corinthians 6:2. Just like Daniel, we pray, not on the basis of our own merits or goodness, but on the basis of God's covenant-keeping faithfulness demonstrated in Jesus' substitutionary death on the cross. It is because of Christ

> We must take responsibility to stand in the gap for our parents' and leaders' sins.

that we can boldly stand before God and ask Him to break the cycle of judgment against our house—"knowing that you were not redeemed with perishable things like silver or gold from your futile way of life inherited from your forefathers, but with precious blood, as of a lamb unblemished and spotless, the blood of Christ" 1 Peter 1:18, 19.

May God help each of us see the promise in the Word, name the sins of our fathers and leaders, repent as intercessors while standing with them, remind God we are there because of His provision at the cross, and begin to receive the divine intervention awaiting us. According to the measure of our repentance, so will He respond.

Imprisoned for Grandpa's Sins

RELATED SCRIPTURES:
Leviticus 26:40-42
2 Samuel 24:17
2 Kings 17:20-23
Nehemiah 9:1-3
Lamentations 5:7
The Book of Daniel, especially Daniel 9:2-19 — *Page 1313*

AND 1 PETER 1:18-19 *Page 1889*

APPLICATIONS:
Describe the difference between individual repentance and corporate repentance.

How might that apply to you or your family? Are there generational curses following you or your children because of ancestor's sins?

Church leaders may need to corporately repent. One church researched its 100-year history and discovered over 40 churches in the city had split off from it. Some had split several times. They wrote letters to all the groups they could identify, offering reconciliation and help. Could your church benefit from their example?

Are you part of a group experiencing God's resistance?

If you are involved in a group with a history of violence, racism, secret rites, or false doctrines, avoid the judgment that results from such association by asking God for mercy for you and your family. Before God, renounce their sins and then take action to separate yourself from them.

Write down Scriptural promises God has given you. Is your faith for their fulfillment increasing? If you've taken a "wait and see" approach, repent and actively pray for their fulfillment.

PRAYER:
Heavenly Father, help me see Your promises in the Bible along with the timing and conditions for their fulfillment. Help me pursue them. Don't let me stay in denial regarding the sins of my relatives and leaders. Empower me to repent as an intercessor. Thank You, Jesus, for Your provision at the cross. Lord, allow me to watch for and embrace Your intervention. Amen.

8

1 TIM 3: 1-7 *Page 1837*

We must establish and keep priorities for stability in our individual and corporate lives.

A 3 Legged Stool won't wobble.

Stability with Gal - Family - Vocation

Spiritual Equipoise

The 3 legged Stool for Retirement - Social Security, Pension, your Personal savings

401 K

I have a sturdy, three-legged stool. Its very structure insures steadiness. Each leg continually connecting with the ground makes the stool wobble proof. Sometimes the pressures of life push us out of balance. That stool is a picture of being "grounded," **establishing and keeping priorities for stability in our individual and corporate lives.**

I realized the "three-legged" concept when I struggled to keep a Christmas tree upright in a stand designed with four stabilizing bolts. It was impossible to evenly adjust the bolts on the uneven tree. I finally removed them, drilled new holes, and placed three bolts in the new locations. The tree stayed upright, without wobbling, held in equilibrium by the three equally-spaced bolts. Likewise, it's impossible for a three-legged stool to wobble.

The U.S. Marine Corps uses groups of threes—three men on a "fire team," three fire teams in a squad with a leader, three squads in a platoon, and three primary tasks per man when on a mission. They have discovered over the years of training men that three of anything works best for levels of command structure as well as for providing the optimum success rate for completing a mission. Fortune 500 companies hire ex-Marines because they know how to get things done.

The secret of success is to get things done without abandoning our other priorities.

**We need a measure of success in our
spiritual life, home, and finances.**

The principles of equilibrium and balancing opposing priorities are found in Scripture. First Timothy 3:1-7 lists qualifications of an "elder" (overseer), traits loosely summarized into three categories: God, family, and vocation (or calling). A leader must have a measure of success in each of these three critical areas.

We may aspire, or actively seek, to be an elder. Scripture speaks of many things we should seek after, or actively pursue, such as love and the gifts of the Spirit: "Pursue love" 1 Corinthians 14:1; "desire earnestly to prophesy" 1 Corinthians 14:39; "earnestly desire the greater gifts" 1 Corinthians 12:31. We should aspire to have the qualities of an elder (1 Timothy 3:1) whether or not a group publicly recognizes us in that official capacity. If we pursue these character traits, we will grow in intimacy with God, mature in our family life, and increase in our finances. Gaining self-control and balance in these areas will position us to exercise authority and bear responsibility in the Kingdom of God and will ultimately earn us recognition from God. We will become like those of whom the Lord said, "Into whatever city ... you enter, inquire who is worthy in it" Matthew 10:11. **From this house the Gospel will go forth with honor and power.** Would the apostles have sought out your home or my home? Would we have been worthy?

Ecc 4:12 A cord of 3 strands is not easily broken.

Our home will be stable in the midst of society's turmoil.

Faith – Hope – Love 1 Thes 1:2

Solomon said, "A cord of three strands is not quickly torn apart" Ecclesiastes 4:12. Just as the symmetry of a natural cord's interaction increases its overall strength, so will the sum of a person's life increase if the three critical areas are balanced. One who does this will stand when others fall, and if he does stumble, he will recover more quickly. **One sign of emotional health is being able to successfully balance priorities that may simultaneously pull us in several directions.**

The first priority is our personal walk with God; second is our relationship with spouse and children (or parents and siblings if still at home); third is our stewardship of money, talents, and calling. **Each one is important, but balancing the three is critical.** Some people have dishonored themselves, their family, and their calling by concentrating so heavily on one of these areas that they neglected one or both of the others. "Taking precaution that no one should discredit us in our administration of this generous gift; for we have regard for what is honorable, not only in the sight of the Lord, but also in the sight of men" 2 Corinthians 8:20, 21.

Love God First –

The most important aspect of one's life is his walk with God. Jesus said, "You shall love the Lord your God with all your heart, ... soul, ... mind, and ... strength" Mark 12:30. This means family and finances are in second and third place. Our love for God should be so strong that, by comparison, our love for family is like hatred. Jesus said, "If anyone comes to Me, and does not hate his own father and mother and wife and

> Our love for God should be so strong that, by comparison, our love for family is like hatred.

children and brother and sister, yes, and even his own life, he cannot be My disciple" Luke 14:26.

We must not mistakenly substitute "ministry" for God. Ministry belongs in the realm of vocation, in third place, after God and family. Some have so loved their ministry, in effect, made it an idol, that they hurt their relationship with God and wounded their family. God, not ministry, must be our passion. It's the only way to be normal. Much religious "weirdness" would be prevented by a healthy commitment to family and friends and productive employment.

Love Jesus first!

Love Jesus first! My heart responds to what He did for me, taking my sin on Himself and offering me His righteousness. Manly fishermen followed Him. Sinners heard Him gladly. Leaders knelt at His feet in worship. Women received release from second-class status when He ministered to them. Children flocked to His open arms, and He told us we should become like them. Jesus feared neither sinner, angry religious hypocrite, nor politician. He caused evil spirits to leave tormented souls. He had time for the hungry and humble. He never sinned. He never worried. He never hurried. He submitted Himself to the cross. His unmatched authority was exceeded only by His unparalleled love. He always listened for His Father's voice and did what He saw His Father doing. He showed us who the Father is and what He is like. Because of who Jesus is, we love Him and put Him first in our lives.

Love your family more than your career.

Our family is next. Scripture says, "Fathers, do not provoke your children to anger; but bring them up in the discipline and instruction of the Lord" Ephesians 6:4.

This involves correction without rejection, instruction without control, and encouragement without license. Love your children more than your reputation. Their behavior may disappoint, humiliate, even sicken us, but while we hate their sin, we continue to love them. We stand by with commitment and hope while they walk through the consequences of their actions. A county judge once told me that in thirty years of court service, the one thing he had learned about parents and teenagers was that parents should never, never, never, never, never, NEVER give up on their kids. God never gives up on us!

God covenanted with us through Jesus, and we covenant with our spouse and children, to lay down our life for them. We provide for them by exposing them to our working faith, by modeling personal life skills, and by encouraging financial soundness. "A good man leaves an inheritance to his children's children" Proverbs 13:22. **This inheritance should encompass the three critical areas.** Too often each generation of young people must build from scratch, without available transitional materials with which to begin their own "houses."

Leave a spiritual, relational, and financial inheritance.

Like Noah, it is the person whose family stands with him who will be mighty in spiritual exploits (Genesis 6:18; 7:1, 13). Building our own family relationships is like Noah's family building the ark. **A strong family will carry us through unfair criticism, unusual circumstances, and unknown storms.** Those lacking natural family should build their "ark" with adopted spiritual kin, their church family.

> Love your children more than your reputation.

ARK

The Family   77   The Church

Create wealth as an assignment from God.

Finally, maintain financial integrity. Apostle Paul modeled balance between competing priorities and used it to teach diligence in service. "For you recall, brethren, our labor and hardship, how working night and day so as not to be a burden to any of you, we proclaimed to you the gospel of God" 1 Thessalonians 2:9. Don't be afraid to get your hands dirty, to work hard to meet pressing needs. Paul was not afraid of extra work, of spending a season "tent-making." He taught financial independence. "Make it your ambition to lead a quiet life and attend to your own business and work with your hands, ... so that you may behave properly toward outsiders and not be in any need" 1 Thessalonians 4:11, 12.

The part about "attend to your own business" could easily mean to have a goal of being self-employed as you have opportunity to become financially free! Create wealth as a stewardship assignment from God. There is no greed in obeying God to pursue a wholesome, clean, and "Kingdom-expanding" idea. It will bless you and everyone around you.

Proper financial stewardship should eventually result in prosperity and rest. It's difficult to handle the "uncertain riches" of this world, but if priorities are balanced, stewarding the ability to make money will bring promotion from God. It is God who gives the power to create wealth (Deuteronomy 8:18), as confirmation of His covenant love. If your assignment is to create spiritual wealth through ministry, then fulfill it in the same way a faithful businessman would create natural wealth.

Create wealth as a stewardship assignment from God.

It is to please and honor Jesus that I share His Gospel, lay down my life for my family, and diligently pursue financial freedom. I must balance these priorities. Keeping them in focus strengthens me and causes me to move toward wholeness. The "three-legged stool" concept provokes me to become "steadfast, immovable, always abounding in the work of the Lord, knowing that your toil is not in vain in the Lord" 1 Corinthians 15:58.

But what about our failures—disobedience to God, broken families, serious indebtedness? If we have experienced such things, can we still achieve a life pleasing to our Lord? Yes! Experiencing and admitting failure qualifies us for God's grace. "It is not those who are healthy who need a physician, but those who are ill" Matthew 9:12.

Experiencing failure qualifies us for God's grace!

If a person proves himself after overcoming tragedy, evidences the Lord's grace in his life, and appears called and equipped by God, how should we receive him? We must have the mind of Christ! Rather than legalistically look at his past, sample the current fruit of his life. **His present character, lifestyle, and direction indicate what's in his heart.** The criterion is not to have matured but to be maturing! Let's face our failures, repent, and determine to mature. We're on the journey! **Thank God for the lessons of brokenness and repentance.** Boast in His grace, not in our goodness.

Paul addressed the subject of dealing with a person's failure in 2 Corinthians 2:6-11. "You should rather forgive and comfort him, lest somehow such a one be overwhelmed by excessive sorrow ... I urge you to reaffirm your love for him ... so that no advantage be taken of us by Satan; for we are not ignorant of his schemes." **Satan's scheme is to trap** the "elder brothers" (Luke 15:25-32) with judgmentalism, to isolate them from experiencing the outpouring of grace upon the restored brother. **We must not fail to forgive those whom God has forgiven!** Rather than find reasons to exclude people, find reasons to include them, to extend grace to them, like Jesus did to us!

Satan schemes to trap the "elder brothers."

Keeping priorities balanced, while graciously responding to others as their lives also mature, makes us more like the Kingdom of God—*unshakable*—Hebrews 12:28. When we have God, family, and vocation in proper order, we can be normal. Christians have been subnormal for so long that when we get normal, people think we're abnormal! With Jesus, let's supernaturally walk in the natural world and naturally walk in the supernatural realm.

Spiritual Equipoise

RELATED SCRIPTURES:
Isaiah 58:9
2 Corinthians 2:7; 7:10
1 Timothy 3:1-15; 6:8-12, 17-21

APPLICATIONS:
If your life were a three-legged stool, would the legs be of equal length? *God, Family? vocation or calling*

If you are not experiencing a measure of success in your spiritual life, home, and finances, what is out of balance? Where can you get help to develop a strategy to correct this?

What practical steps can you take to build or strengthen the areas of your life that are lacking? Name something you can do immediately.

What can you do that requires long-term planning? What are the initial steps toward that goal? Can you develop small milestones to measure your success as you change the priorities in your life?

Have you "elder brothered" someone? Did you apply legalism, criticism, or overly-harsh standards toward someone who stumbled? How can you release him once he has repented?

Do you know someone who is overwhelmed by "excessive sorrow" for his past? Do you think God wants him to stay in that condition? What can you do to help?
(Note: Churches are full of such people.)

PRAYER:

Heavenly Father, thank You for the lessons of brokenness and repentance. Thank You for Your grace. Help me forgive those whom You've forgiven. I trust You to direct me into a godly life with balanced priorities. I love You first, Jesus. Show me how to build a strong "ark" with my family. Help me maintain financial integrity by faithfully stewarding my abilities and gifts so that my work is fruitful. Make me unshakable, Lord. Thank You. Amen.

9

God Himself will intervene.

Plan A
Plan B
Plan C

The ABCs of Fatherhood

The Absence of a father is TRAGIC

God's Plan "A" for families is for the fathers to "bring them [their children] up in the discipline and instruction of the Lord" Ephesians 6:4. This doesn't always happen, due to ignorance, willful disobedience, or tragic circumstances. Strangely enough, many Christian leaders no longer view the absence of fathering as tragic but rather as a normal way of parenting in today's home. Some Christian leaders even believe there is no longer any such thing as a "normal" family. But God's nature is to create families, and He has provisions for when they fail.

God has a backup plan—Plan "B"—in which elders fulfill the patriarchal role model in the church. These leaders serve as a shelter for widows and orphans, as well as a storehouse of information and resources for the hurting, lonely, abandoned, or weak in faith (Ezekiel 33:1-5). As pillars in the house of God, they provide shade from the heat of the day and protection from the storms of life for all who look to the Lord.

An example of how God sends someone to our rescue is Leviticus 25:47. "If a ... countryman of yours becomes so poor

... as to sell himself to a stranger, ... One of his brothers may redeem him, ... or if he prospers, he may redeem himself." So, there was a plan for intervention when hardship came into a brother's life. But God's instructions went even further; **He planned for the unfortunate brother's release even if the brother's kinsmen or countrymen did not help.** "Even if he is not redeemed by these means, he shall still go out in the year of jubilee, he and his sons with him. For the sons of Israel are My servants; they are My servants whom I brought out from the land of Egypt. I am the Lord your God" Leviticus 25:54, 55.

In the church, the elders are to see to it that the weak and captive have someone caring for them. Watching over the flock, they look for the ones experiencing hardship, separation, or discouragement. At special risk are the fatherless, divorcees, widows, and families led by "absentee fathers"—there physically but "AWOL" spiritually.

The prime Biblical example of an elder is Job. Job 29 and 31 reveal Job's manly compassion and loyalty to both his neighbors and his family. He was a man's man and a godly man. He "was the greatest of all the men of the east" Job 1:3. He interceded for his sons. "Job would send and consecrate them, rising up early in the morning and offering burnt offerings ... for Job said, 'Perhaps my sons have sinned and cursed God in their hearts.' Thus Job did continually" Job 1:5. **Job interceded in prayer for his family.**

His honor and standing in the community matched the requirements in the church that an elder "must have a good reputation with those outside the church" 1 Timothy 3:7. "When I went out to the gate of the city, when I took my seat in the square; the young men saw me and hid themselves, and the old men arose and stood. The princes stopped talking, and put their hands on their mouths" Job 29:7-9. **Job had a good reputation.**

Job said, "I delivered the poor who cried for help, and the orphan who had no helper. The blessing of the one ready to perish came upon me, and I made the widow's heart sing for joy. ... I was a father to the needy, and I investigated the case which I did not know, and I broke the jaws of the wicked" Job 29:12-17. **Job had a father's heart.**

Furthermore, Job's integrity as a leader is revealed in his secret life. "I have made a covenant with my eyes; How then could I gaze at a virgin?" Job 31:1. **Job walked in personal integrity.** He would never have subscribed to Internet pornography.

"If I have gloated because my wealth was great, And because my hand had secured so much ... I would have denied God above" Job 31:25, 28. Though Job was wealthy beyond measure, **Job was free from the love of money.**

"If I have looked at the sun when it shone, or the moon going in splendor, and my heart became secretly enticed, and my hand threw a kiss from my mouth, that too would have been an iniquity calling for judgment, for I would have denied God above" Job 31:26-28. **Job did not secretly indulge in astrology or horoscopes.** He would never have called the "psychic hot line."

He even treated his employees respectfully. "If I have despised the claim of my male or female slaves when they filed a complaint against me, what then could I do when God arises, and when He calls me to account, what will I answer Him? Did not He who made me in the womb make him, and the same one fashion us in the womb?" Job 31:13-15. **Job treated people with respect because God created each person.**

He was a shelter for those weaker and less fortunate and a model of integrity. **Society needs men like Job. Churches need men like Job.** The church must comprehend the depth of God's commitment to the helpless and, rather than just institute programs, build men with the character of Job. **God desires to raise up millionaires with absolute integrity.** Job was such a man! The church must pray them in, disciple them when they show up, and challenge our own sons in the faith to prosper as never before!

While programs are part of the answer, none of them function beyond the point of their empowerment. **A program can be no better than the heart of its leader.** If the Father's heart is not energizing and directing each leader, then the result is just another bureaucracy with a church label on it. **Such programs function only as "spiritual orphanages" until God raises up fathers in the faith.**

At some point, God will take matters into His own hands. "Then I myself shall gather the remnant of My flock ... I shall also raise up shepherds over them and they will tend them; and they will not be ... terrified, nor will any be missing" Jeremiah 23:3, 4.

> **God desires to raise up millionaires with absolute integrity.**

Even if all those in leadership fail to obey, God still has Plan "C." No one will be left to the mercy of the devil's plans to steal, kill, and destroy. Even the smallest child can call on the Lord for help. David, the young shepherd boy, before he was king, was rejected by his own parents when the prophet came to his house. They sent him away with the sheep and presented all their other sons to the prophet. David later wrote, "Though my father and mother forsake me, the Lord will receive me" Psalm 27:10 NIV.

The youngest believer can appeal to a Higher Authority for assistance. God Himself will intervene. He is a Heavenly Father to all who call Jesus "Lord." He taught us to pray, "Our Father, who art in Heaven … " Matthew 6:9.

I have taught my four sons that if anything ever happens to their mother or me, **the most important thing in the world is to know how to pray.** You see, there is a Father on the throne of the universe who loves them even more than I do. He is ready and able to intervene in their behalf if I am unable to complete my assignment as their father.

God will judge those of us who deliberately fail to care for the next generation. To abandon, neglect, or refuse to provide nurture and resources is to offend the little ones assigned to our care. "And He called a child to Himself and stood him in their midst, and said, … 'whoever causes one of these little ones who believe in Me to stumble, it is better for him that a heavy millstone be hung around his neck, and that he be drowned in the depth of the sea'" Matthew 18:2, 6. **If you are an "absentee father," you have already offended your little ones.**

The American church needs clean, godly millionaires like Job! A businessman told me that all the wealthy acquaintances he knew engaged in promiscuous activity when they traveled. The life of Job is a challenge to every millionaire, that he can both steward great wealth and walk clean!

Judgment also awaits us if we fail to keep our responsibilities as leaders or ministers of the Gospel. "'Woe to the shepherds who are destroying and scattering the sheep of My pasture ... I am about to attend to you for the evil of your deeds,' declares the Lord" Jeremiah 23:1, 2. Being a Christian, especially a Christian leader, carries definite responsibilities for which God holds us accountable.

If Plan "A" was never implemented for you by loving parents in a secure home and Plan "B" was overlooked by the church, then call on God. He has Plan "C" for you. "'I [the Lord] will welcome you. And I will be a Father to you, And you shall be sons and daughters to Me,' says the Lord Almighty" 2 Corinthians 6:17, 18. God not only rules, He overrules! He is a Father! **For those who have no one to turn to, God is the Father of last resort.** Call on Him!

We cannot control what life gives us, but we needn't remain a victim. We can appeal to God. He will make up the difference and even go beyond what we would have received in the natural.

Turn to Him today with your whole heart, trusting that, in Christ at Calvary, He provided everything you need to be His child and receive His best. If you got down off your daddy's lap too soon, **climb up on Father God's lap today, and let Him finish the job of fathering your soul.**

The ABCs of Fatherhood

RELATED SCRIPTURES:
Job 29:1-17
Psalm 112
Isaiah 1:16, 17
Zechariah 7:9, 10
Malachi 4:6
James 1:27

APPLICATIONS:
If you weren't reared in a Plan "A" family,

> forgive those who failed you.

> acknowledge problems in your life due to improper parenting.

> pray for your own healing and release.

> ask the Lord to mentor you as a father would.

Some parents are worthy of great honor, but all are worthy of some honor. If you can't honor them due to their behavior, at least honor the office of parent they hold. In what ways can you show a proper measure of honor?

Put families on your prayer list. Pray for an increase of healthy families. Ask God to strengthen and encourage faithful moms and dads. Ask Him to help build connections between generations.

Pray for the church elders who serve as a shelter and a storehouse to those in need. If such a person was instrumental in your life, pray the Lord will bless him or her.

Study Job's character traits found in this chapter. Place an "x" by Job's characteristics that you are walking in.

Do you believe it is possible to be both godly and manly?

Do you believe it is possible to be both godly and wealthy?

Read James 5:11. What is the outcome of the Lord's dealings with you?

PRAYER:
Heavenly Father, I forgive and release those who failed to fulfill their responsibilities in my life. I ask You to heal my wounds, dismantle my defenses, and change my circumstances. Finish the job of fathering my soul. Lord God, please forgive me where I have failed as a father and leader. I desire to be a faithful man with my children, my church family, and the fatherless. Thank You, Father. Amen.

10

*Let's live in such a way that
we build happy memories for our kids.*

Paint Your Own
Norman Rockwell

umerous events have convinced us that our family
is different from the norm. One situation occurred
shortly after we moved into a house with a huge oak
tree in the yard. Our boys, then ages 1, 3, 6, and 9, immediately
requested a tree fort. Before I get to the actual point of this
story, let me digress with a sad-but-true confession.

In my quest to be a first class dad, I sometimes get off
track. This was one of those times. I had just earned my
Florida General Contractor's License and had many Texas
construction projects under my belt. I couldn't build just a
fort; I had to design and construct "the mother of all tree
forts." I envisioned a two-story structure with a balcony and
lookout tower. (Wanting to keep it simple, I would put off
the drawbridge and moat for Phase II.) Unfortunately, due to
a lack of time and money for a project of this magnitude, the
fort's ground breaking kept being delayed.

One lovely spring afternoon, my wife Kay, who,
incidentally, had no official sanction by the licensing
board of the state of Florida, decided to build the fort. She
gathered up some scrap lumber left from the construction

of our home, grabbed my hammer, saw, and nails, and went to work.

When I arrived home a few hours later, the fruit of her best efforts caught my attention loud and clear. It wasn't the simple little platforms she'd managed to wedge into the branches or the primitive slat ladder climbing up the trunk. It was the sheer delight written ear-to-ear across our sons' faces. Indeed, we had the MOTHER of all tree forts—just not the way I had imagined.

While I'm proud of my wife, I still feel the twinge of regret because I missed this chance to fulfill our boys' dreams. It would have been better for me to downsize than to postpone and disappoint.

Now, back to the main story. One of our neighbors, Lee, a widow in her 60s, was out walking when Kay and the boys were in the middle of their project. She heard the ring of the hammer and the rasp of the saw, but what caught her attention was the excited little boys running around, eagerly shouting into the tree, "Can we come up?" "Are you almost finished?" Unable to suppress her curiosity, Lee marched across the yard and, spotting Kay amongst the branches, introduced herself with the question, "What in the world are you doing?"

Along with the tree fort explanation, Kay shared about our then home schooling family, and each of the boys added his own story about "Life in the Woods." Eyes wide with interest, Lee groped for the right words to express her feelings. Finally, looking all about her, she said, "This reminds me of a Norman Rockwell painting." In her mind, we didn't act or look like the current average family; we reflected memories from her past.

Listen to the words from Zechariah 8:4, 5—"Thus says the Lord of Hosts, old men and old women will again sit in the streets of Jerusalem, each man with his staff in his hand because of age. And the streets of the city will be filled with boys and girls playing in its streets." God speaks of a time when elders will again reside in a safe place and children will play happily and safely in the streets. Times of blessing from God are indicated by safe homes and peaceful neighborhoods.

Many have observed the disappearance of the innocence of childhood. Crime, abandonment, poverty, pornography, and overworked adults all contribute to rob children of their childhood. The same forces work to rob grandparents of their rightful role as elders in a society that desperately needs a sense of continuity.

The Israelites got themselves into a place of judgment because "just as He called and they would not listen, so they called and I would not listen,' says the Lord of Hosts" Zechariah 7:13. Today's society is squeezed by economic and social pressures because of a failure to heed the prophetic call from men of God. There is a place for both individual and corporate repentance. **Each of us facing insurmountable time and money pressures would do well to turn to God with a humble heart and a determination to hear His voice.**

I am motivated to do so. I desire to hear the sound of boys and girls playing in the streets with joy, in safety, and with a sense of God's favor and blessing. Later, I want to take my place with the old men who have labored and who now observe the generation coming after them.

> Times of blessing from God are indicated by safe homes and peaceful neighborhoods.

93

Years after initially writing this chapter, I heard Rush Limbaugh, the most widely listened to radio talk show host in America, speaking about his grandfather—a patriarch whose values, integrity, and dignity enabled the family, for the most part, to live a Norman Rockwell painting.

Let's live in such a way that we build happy memories for both our kids and our grandkids. Let's keep them talking about us after we are gone.

By the way, tree forts don't have to cost a lot of time or money. An enormous, sturdy wood-and-wire crate found by the side of the road and pulled into the upper branches of that ole' tree made it a two-story fort after all. While it never had a drawbridge, it did have strategically placed ropes for quick escapes and exhilarating swings through the air.

Our Heavenly Father has commissioned each of us, in our unique way, to "paint our own Norman Rockwell." Don't wait on someone else to paint your picture for you. Get engaged. Pick up your brush and begin to paint on the canvas God has given you. "Do the stuff!"

Paint Your Own Norman Rockwell

RELATED SCRIPTURES:
Deuteronomy 6:7
Psalms 92:12-14; 127; 128; 133:1, 3; 144:12-15
Proverbs 17:6
Zechariah 8:1-5
Mark 10:14, 16

APPLICATIONS:
Do you have any "Norman Rockwells" from your childhood? Have you had any times like that with your kids? Describe them.

Do you think Jesus had moments like that with His disciples?

If your family life was dysfunctional or non-existent, do you have friends with wholesome families to whom you can look for a pattern of success?

Do you believe God desires for you to have a normal family? Why?

What is God's remedy for loneliness?

What projects might God be nudging you to "downsize rather than postpone and disappoint"? Can you begin now?

What ideas do you have for building happy memories for your family?

How could you include your kids' friends who have single parents?

PRAYER:
    Heavenly Father, please help me set aside time to turn to You with a humble heart and hear Your voice. Instruct me in my fathering roll. Sensitize me to the needs around me which You intend for me to meet. Enable me to build happy memories. Refresh me with joyful memories with You, so that I can refresh others. Thank You, Lord. Amen.

11

*Men with integrity are God's
back-up plan for fatherlessness.*

Stand in the Gap

S ome years ago, my wife Kay worked on an interior decorating project that involved hand sawing some boards. She said she learned her skills as a child, "helping" her dad with various projects. Before I knew what was happening, her eyes filled with tears. Although her dad had then been dead 35 years, her heart still felt the pain of his absence.

She had been his shadow. She sipped "kid's coffee" with him before his early morning departure for work and met him at the door upon his return. After dinner, with Kay atop the push plow, they headed off to the garden. She kept him company when he chopped wood. They played baseball together. He'd hit; she'd catch—barehanded so he'd be really proud of her. They had a special worm-digging system for their fishing trips. He placed the spade upright on the ground; she jumped on its top edge, pushing it down; he scooped up the dirt; she grabbed the worms and plunked them in the dirt-filled Folgers coffee can. (Talk about patience! This man enjoyed his little girl!) He built her a swing set. He paid her a quarter to pick stick tights off his hunting clothes. He played—cards, hide-and-seek, board games. He teased her and called her nicknames. Way too soon, when Kay was only twelve, surgery revealed cancer, and he died three months later.

We all know someone who has lost a father. Believe it or not, disease or accident may be the "easier" way to lose a parent. There is no rejection or betrayal in death—it just hurts. The pain is very real. The emotional and financial loss is immediate and sometimes profound. Abandonment or divorce, however, adds to the pain of loss the additional pain of failure, betrayal, broken promises, ongoing rejection, and shame. Regardless of the cause of the loss, those left behind need healing and special attention.

A dad has an important function in his child's life. Done right, as in Kay's situation, it's a very active role, a daily opportunity to teach, love, enjoy, labor alongside, and encourage. When her father died, a huge void was left in her life. It was critical for her self-esteem and wellbeing for some godly, caring men to "stand in the gap."

There are numerous Biblical examples of men who stood in when the father figure was missing or when extra manly care and encouragement was needed. **Abram was that kind of man for his nephew Lot.** When he left Ur for Canaan, Abram took Lot with him. When the land could no longer sustain all their flocks, herds, and tents, Abram, the peacemaker, gave Lot first choice of the land. Later, when God revealed His plan to destroy Sodom and Gomorrah, Abram interceded on Lot's behalf, saving his life (Genesis 12:5; 13:6-9; 19:29). Abram **guided, provided for, and rescued** Lot.

Mordecai accepted parental responsibility for an orphan. "He was bringing up Hadassah, that is Esther, his uncle's daughter, for she had no mother or father. Now the young lady was beautiful of form and face, and when her father and her mother died, Mordecai took her as his own daughter" Esther 2:7. He watched out for her, even after she had left his home. He prayed and fasted for her while she acted on his wise counsel in a life-and-death situation. Mordecai **prepared, strengthened, and inspired** Esther, enabling her to save her people. *VEGETALES -has A Story About ESTER,*

Job was a tremendous model of manliness and tenderness. Orphans, strangers, underdogs, and the dying **felt his compassion, tasted his provision, and benefited from his protection.** "I was eyes to the blind, and feet to the lame. I was a father to the needy" Job 29:15-16.

Paul took Timothy under his care as a "son in the faith," supporting and building upon the preparatory work his grandmother Lois and his mother Eunice had already done. He encouraged, admonished, invested in, and recommended Timothy, **empowering and releasing him into his life's work** (1 Timothy - 2 Timothy).

At the foot of the cross at Calvary, Apostle **John became a "stand in" to care for Jesus' bereaved mother,** Mary. "When Jesus ... saw His mother, and the disciple whom He loved standing nearby, He said to His mother, 'Woman, behold, your son!' Then He said to the disciple, 'Behold, your mother!' And from that hour the disciple **took her into his own household**" John 19:26, 27.

God Himself steps in to care for the abandoned and needy. **"A father of the fatherless and a judge for the widows, is God in His holy habitation"** Psalm 68:5. "The Lord protects the strangers; He supports the fatherless and the widow" Psalm 146:9. "'Then I will draw near to you for judgment; and I will be a swift witness against the sorcerers and against the

We took sermon Tapes to shut ins. The best part was befriending/ loving the old people.

adulterers and against those who swear falsely, and against those who oppress the wage earner in his wages, the widow and the orphan, and those who turn aside the alien, and do not fear Me,' says the Lord of hosts" Malachi 3:5.

After her daddy's death, Kay's uncle invited her to join his family on a fishing trip. She had really missed going fishing. It was a marvelous day, and she was blessed. Her uncle **stood in for his brother** for the sake of his niece.

Kay's high school graduation came with activities and honors—her dad would have been so proud. To fill the void his absence created, a special man went out of his way. Kay's older brother, stationed with the Air Force in California, caught a cargo plane for a brief stopover in Kansas **to be there** for his sister. Imagine her surprise, seeing him in uniform, full of pride and devotion. It was just what she needed.

Another man played a vital role in Kay's life—her stepfather. He committed to love and provide for not only Kay's mother, but also for Kay and her two brothers. He did this faithfully and honorably. Kay never feared that he would take advantage of her or that he had less than her best interest in mind. He wasn't a replacement for her father but rather **an extension of her father's influence and care.**

> God Himself steps in to care for the abandoned and needy.

Kay benefited from both **a professional and spiritual mentor.** Her supervising teacher encouraged and guided her through the student teaching, job application, and beginning career process. He provided instruction and direction for this important transitional phase of her life. In addition, he provoked her toward a renewed commitment to her Heavenly Father and drew her into fellowship with an extended family of Christian brothers and sisters, many who are still very close to her.

Another man played a fatherly role in her life. A pastor who knew both Kay and me felt "nudged" by God to arrange, behind the scenes, for us to meet. It was 10 years before we knew of his involvement. Married over 25 years, we are convinced this man represented the Father's heart to us. "God sets the lonely in families" Psalm 68:6.

All around us are opportunities to stand in the gap as the Father's representative. Years ago, a young man, Pete, sought refuge with our family because of a difficult home situation. We couldn't change his dad, but as we endeavored to model godly family life to Pete—forgiveness, love, encouragement, faith in Jesus—his paradigm of fatherhood changed. Instead of a legalistic and demanding God, Pete began to perceive Him as Someone who loved him and was excited about him. "The Lord your God is in your midst, a victorious warrior. He will exult over you with joy, He will be quiet in His love, He will rejoice over you with shouts of joy" Zephaniah 3:17. Discovering how God viewed him and accepting God's fathering helped Pete grow into a happier, healthier, more confident young man. With this revelation and fresh identity, Pete was able to forgive, return home, and relate with his natural dad.

Many people are like Pete—they could achieve great things if only someone demonstrated the Father's love to them. Pete's father didn't change, but Pete did. Given a choice, most kids will live with an abusive parent rather than have no parent at all; any father is better than none. We long for our father.

Let's have special concern for the fatherless in our areas of influence—Little League, school, church, neighborhood, business—we should be mindful of the void we can fill in the lives of those who are fatherless. **Someone around us is looking for his father—how we respond could lead him to his Heavenly Father.** We must have the Father's heart. Somebody is watching us. God is watching, too, looking for men of integrity to represent Him in the lives of His children—both young and old. Let's look for opportunities to stand in the gap!

Stand in the Gap

RELATED SCRIPTURES:
The book of Esther
Matthew 1:18-25 *Joseph didn't put Mary away when she was pregnant with Jesus.*

APPLICATIONS:
Mordecai cared for Esther after her parents died (Esther 2:7). Did people other than your parents play an important role in your life? What did they contribute to you?

———

Mordecai was promoted to second to the king as a result of the turn of events (Esther 10:3). How might God promote you if you are faithful to a fatherless generation?

What young leaders can you befriend in order to influence them for godly purposes?

The most famous person to rear someone else's son was Joseph, Mary's husband. What are the ramifications of Joseph's obedience?

PRAYER:
Heavenly Father, You have adopted me. You have taken me into Your family, even when I wasn't very compatible with You. I have benefited from Your patient care and oversight. Help me be patient and loyal toward those You send to me who also need Your love. Thank You for making me a part of Your eternal family. Thank You for the inheritance You have set aside for me. Amen.

12

*Our failures are not enough
to prevent our maturing into
the things of God.*

Don't You Dare Give Up!

I mplicit in manhood is endurance and an ability to face consequences. Scripture tells us to "act like men" 1 Corinthians 16:13. Even in God's presence, men are told to stand on their feet and talk to Him "like a man" Job 38:3. And again, in the face of the enemy of our soul, we are told, "Having done all, stand" Ephesians 6:13.

Sometimes we don't feel like standing. Nothing in us wants to stand. But courage comes from being with God. "On the day I called Thou didst answer me; Thou didst make me bold with strength in my soul" Psalm 138:3. When we are hard pressed, if we will humble ourselves before God, He will give us courage and stand us on our feet, and we will always come through. Some situations are so painful that just enduring is itself a victory.

An elderly apostle in the faith shared a bit of wisdom with me that we should all embrace. It is simply this: **"In spiritual warfare, he who fights, wins."** God said, "Resist the devil and he will flee from you" James 4:7. If we don't resist him, the devil wins. If we do resist him, we win. It's that simple.

Sometimes it is a fight to let go of something, to yield to God's plan. Our flesh wants to hold on to some thing, person, or circumstance that God is changing. Letting go is a "faith fight." When David's son from his affair with Bathsheba died, David arose from seven days of prayer, bathed, changed his garments, and came into the house of God and worshipped. He yielded to God's decision. He'd said, "Who knows, the Lord may be gracious to me, that the child may live. But now he has died; why should I fast? Can I bring him back again? I shall go to him, but he will not return to me" 2 Samuel 12:22, 23. **The grace of yielding is a test of standing spiritually.**

Most of our tests are not so severe. They are more in the nature of pressure from several sources: stressful schedules, financial hardship, home difficulties, career setbacks, health problems. It could be as major as a job change or relocation or as minor as a misunderstanding with family or friends.

It is unrealistic to expect everything to always go perfectly just because we are following Jesus. **God sometimes calls us to walk with Him in settings and circumstances we do not fully understand.** Because we won't always look successful, especially to people with a religious mindset, we must learn to throw off "religious expectations."

In the midst of great pressures, don't allow your hunger for God to be diverted to religious weirdness. It's important to continue to be a caring husband, a good dad, a faithful friend, and an effective steward of our business skills. Excessive religious devotion that doesn't produce life in our family or prosperity in our business is possibly a step toward "religious weirdness."

Don't be pressed into a religious mold. Even though we are called into ministry, God may want us to be bi-vocational.

"The whole earth is full of His glory" Isaiah 6:3. We probably have skills in many areas; using those skills will glorify God and not hurt our spirituality. There's a proper balance. The Puritans, the early founders of the Colonies that became the United States of America, understood the sanctity of work and declared the dignity of all legitimate work. Their legacy had a profound impact on our fledgling nation.

Associate with men of strength and draw from their experiences and perspectives. Find men with whom you can both share and receive (avoid "one-way" relationships). Read biographies of men who endured and succeeded in difficult times—men like Winston Churchill, Martin Luther, Theodore Roosevelt, Abraham Lincoln, Ronald Reagan, Stanley Livingston, and Martin Luther King. They made it; so can we. They may not have been perfect, but they had a profound impact.

Don't allow problems to so weigh you down that you fail to exercise initiative. Pressures of life sometimes cause husbands and fathers to retreat into despondency. Keep up the initiative at home for wholesome activities; continue building warm family memories.

A father's faithful, steadfast love drives out the "ites" that would otherwise inhabit the land of our family's soul. Our fatherhood, under God's leadership, will drive out Jezebel spirits, rebellion, unbelief, and every other enemy of Christ's Spirit. "Love never fails" 1 Corinthians 13:8. It won't fail in our home either. Fatherly love is love that initiates. It moves in to fill the emptiness in our spouse and in our children.

> Let's not allow problems to so weigh us down that we fail to exercise initiative.

Study the Scriptures on God's dealing in hard times. He uses such seasons to discipline, judge, redirect, and begin restoration. Read Jeremiah, Ezekiel, and Lamentations and find personal applications.

Sometimes it just takes a little time for our life to settle down to a level where we have a comfortable degree of success in the crucial areas of existence—knowing God, loving our family, and enjoying who we are. From that foundation, we can rebuild in order to reach our other goals. When pressed on all sides, endeavor to do what really matters instead of just what is urgent.

Remember, God loves us like a daddy loves his son or daughter—not just the way any dad loves any child, but the way the Father loved Jesus (John 17:26). He won't let us go. He won't give us more than we can bear, but He will stretch us. In that stretching, we will learn that our strength must come from Him, not from ourselves. He won't grow discouraged with us while He works on us. **He is able. He cares for us. He is presently at work in our lives.**

Don't you dare give up! God is always there! He has great plans for you. He loves you with a love that won't quit. If you are honest with God and keep looking to Him, even when you fail, **He won't quit showing His kindness in tangible ways. He won't quit planning good things for you. He won't grow tired of you.** You'll endure if you keep looking ahead. You'll eventually see the fruit of walking with God. "No discipline seems pleasant at the time, but painful. Later on, however, it produces

> Don't you dare give up! God is always there! He has great plans for you. He loves you with a love that won't quit.

a harvest of righteousness and peace for those who have been trained by it" Hebrews 12:11.

How can it be that God would demonstrate such loyalty to us? He prepared us for "Life with Father" by the work of Jesus on the cross. All the punishment due us was placed on Jesus so that all the good due Him could be made available to us. Judgment was certainly coming to us, in this life and in the next, but we escape it if we are Christ's. When we change our heart and our most deeply held beliefs, yield our stubborn mind to Him, begin to believe and say what God says about us and His work on the cross, a spiritual change takes place in our inner man.

We must see Him bearing away all our sin and unworthiness, see ourselves as a part of Christ—holy, just, joined with Him in ruling the universe from the throne of God, free from sin.

We must change our "self-talk," the negative evaluations of ourselves and our circumstances. We tend to continually flood our mind with old images of ourselves instead of speaking what God says about us. Proclaim what He has said in His Word and whispered in our ear. Say it to ourselves and others. It will change the atmosphere around us.

We were created to be sons of God, born again into His family. We were called to steward ourselves, our family, our work, and our part of this world. We receive God's provision as His Kingdom increases in every realm of our life. It grows in our heart, our home, and our business.

Our past failures are not bad enough to prevent our maturing into the things of God. They were not bad enough to keep Jesus in the tomb! Our weakness in the present gives way to His life-giving power working in us even now. It's not too good to be true. It's too good to be the devil! "For it is God who is at work in you, both to will and to work for His good pleasure" Philippians 2:13.

We may have made a start only to have suffered a setback. Remember, the Lord said, "My strength is made perfect in weakness" 2 Corinthians 12:9. That project you started—pick it up again. That phone call or visit you never made—make it now. Start your exercise program, make a date with your wife and kids, find that quiet, personal time with God you promised yourself. Begin to do what God created you to do. **Life is full of detours; don't allow them to become stop signs.**

Three Days from the Kingdom

Sometimes the most difficult battles come just days before the greatest victories. That happened to a shepherd boy who was the victim of a jealous king's relentless assassination attempts. At a place called Ziklag, the wives and children of David and his men were captured and their camp burned while the men were away in battle. It was David's darkest hour. Even though his men taunted him and threatened to stone him, David encouraged himself in the Lord his God. He went on to recover every family member and all their possessions. Little did he know that three days later, he would be anointed king of Israel (1 Samuel 30 - 2 Samuel 2).

When Jesus died on the cross, He laid down His own life, crying, "It is finished!" John 19:30. On the third day, He was raised from the dead on the basis of His own shed blood. Even the tomb was not the end.

It may be our darkest hour—the persecution, the financial failure, the family misunderstanding, the taunts and threats by former friends. There may be no apparent way out, but let's do what David did—**encourage ourselves in the Lord our God!** We, too, may be only three days from victory!

"Blessed is the man who perseveres under trial, because when he has stood the test, he will receive the crown of life that God has promised to those who love Him" James 1:12.

Wait in God's presence. Repent and embrace correction. Strengthen what you can. Do the basics with your family now. Proclaim God's Word to yourself—literally talk to yourself. Expectantly seek God for wisdom for your vocation. Listen to God and do what He tells you.

God knows the way. He has a plan to reveal. Ask, listen, watch, and respond.

Don't You Dare Give Up!

RELATED SCRIPTURES:
1 Samuel 30:6
Matthew 26:41
Romans 8:28-39
1 Corinthians 9:24-27
2 Corinthians 6:4
Philippians 3:12-14
2 Timothy 2:1-7
Hebrews 12:1

APPLICATIONS:
Name areas of discipline that seemed painful yet produced positive results in your life.

What kinds of "things" will you overwhelmingly conquer (Romans 8:37)?

What has God said in His Word and whispered in your ear about you?

Name an area in which God desires you to take the initiative in order to fill an empty space in your family.

What steps will you take to do this?

How can you encourage yourself in the Lord?

PRAYER:

Heavenly Father, thank You that my past failures are not bad enough to prevent my maturing into the things You have for me. I repent for my sins. I embrace Your correction. Lord, I desire to encourage myself in You! I'm asking for Your plan. Help me to listen faithfully and watch expectantly for Your answer. Help me to respond in faith, believing. Amen.

PART THREE

GENERATIONAL
TRANSFER

*Blessing our offspring
creates opportunities to
share the heart of God.*

OUR AMBASSITOR FOR CHRIST -
God BACKS UP HIS AMBASSIDORS AS AMERICA
BACKS UP THEIR AMBASSIDORS.

KY BACKS UP THEIR POLICEMEN.

Blessing means well WORDS

Authority to Bless SANCTFIED

John 17:18- Jesus said - As the father has sent me
UNTO The WORLD - I HAVE sent them into the world.
P 1631

J esus was asked, "By what authority are You doing these
things, and who gave You this authority?" Matthew
21:23. Sometimes it is others, but most often it is you
and me, questioning our own authority. Knowing our measure
of authority is important to accomplishing God's will.

You have no greater authority than when you operate
in the realm of your own calling. Within your sphere, your
words have power. You have confidence when you know you
are within your realm.

If you have a wife, you are called to be a husband. If
you have kids, you are called to be a father. If you have a
congregation, you are called to be a teacher and protector. If
you have a business, you are called to be a mentor. Make full
proof of your calling in all arenas (2 Timothy 4:5).

Several years ago, Kay and I were in the home of a young
couple that had just suffered the miscarriage of their first
pregnancy. The wife was still deeply grieving the loss, and
her husband didn't know how to help her break free of the

depression. Kay and I prayed with them, then we encouraged him to stand firmly in his position as head of the home, as husband, and speak a blessing over his wife. "Blessing" means "well-words."

He wrapped his arms around her, held her tight, and prayed, "God, I bless my wife. I bless her femininity. I bless her womb. I bless her desire to be a mother. And I ask You to bless her, Lord." Literally, a spirit of joy came over her. Tears of sadness gave way to laughter and then praise. About nine months later, this formerly heartbroken woman gave birth to a healthy boy! Praise God! **"The effective prayer of a righteous man can accomplish much"** James 5:16.

There is a Scriptural precedent for imparting the blessing. God uses His people to accomplish His purposes. Here are examples:

God blessed Adam and Eve.	Genesis 1:27-31
Melchizedek blessed Abram.	Genesis 14:17-20
God blessed Abraham.	Genesis 22:17, 18
Abraham blessed Isaac. (implied)	Genesis 24:7; 25:5, 11; 26:24; 28:4
Bethuel and Laban blessed Rebekah.	Genesis 24:60
Isaac (and God) blessed Jacob.	Genesis 27:7, 12; 28:1-4; Hebrews 11:20
Jacob blessed Joseph.	Genesis 48:15-22
Jacob blessed grandkids.	Genesis 48:15-22; Hebrews 11:21
Jacob blessed all the tribes of Israel.	Genesis 49:1-28, esp. 25-28
Joseph commissioned a generation.	Genesis 50:23-26
Aaron was to bless Israel.	Numbers 6:22-27
Priests were chosen to bless Israel.	Deuteronomy 21:5

Moses blessed all the tribes.	Deuteronomy 33:1-34:5
David blessed all the people.	1 Chronicles 16:2
David blessed his own household.	1 Chronicles 16:43
Jesus blessed the children.	Mark 10:13-16
Jesus blessed the disciples.	Luke 24:50-52

These men spoke words of blessing over people they were commissioned by God to serve. **It is a duty to bless in the Name of the Lord.**

The **purpose of the blessing** is that all the earth might taste the grace of God and come to know Him. "All the nations of the earth will be blessed" Genesis 18:18; "All the nations [families] shall be blessed" Genesis 22:18. We are called to bless, not to curse.

Fathers are called to bless, intercede, and worship in the presence of God. They stand before God in prayer for their family, not just for themselves.

Repeatedly, Old Testament saints and priests blessed in the Name of the Lord. Now, with the priesthood of every believer, we can all stand and bless.

Who are you to bless your own family? Don't wait for a minister to do what you are commissioned by God to do. God does indeed call elders to stand in the gap and bless, but as a husband and father, you, first, are called to exercise faith and speak words of blessing over your family. James 5:17 illustrates having faith in spite of personal weaknesses— "Elijah was a man with a nature like ours, and he prayed earnestly that it might not rain; and it did not rain on the earth for three years and six months." Use your faith to fight your fear and discomfort of leadership.

The principle of blessing that works for fathers also works for mothers. Mom, if there is no father in your child's life, you take a stand. As a young teenager, I went to Mom after weeks of unsuccessfully wrestling with fear and anxiety attacks. My heart raced, and it felt like a tight band was constricting around my head. Mom pulled me close and prayed, interceding in the Spirit. Then **she prayed over me in the Name of Jesus, recounting the power of His blood. As she prayed, peace entered my body,** beginning at the top of my head and going all the way to my feet. Fear washed out of my body. The band of pressure left. Jesus delivered me from that torment when Mom prayed. Be a "Deborah" (Judges 4, 5), take courage, and go for it! God will answer you.

The devil attempts to disqualify and discourage us. Our relatives may inadvertently crush our faith. Our own soul seeks to impeach us before God. We must obey God, rather than man, in the exercise of our authority to bless.

Speak words of blessing! Speak blessings with daily devotions, at bedtime with the kids. Give "impromptu blessings"—grab a kid, give a quick word of encouragement, and let him go. I call this "Blessing en Passant."

Write out blessings on birthdays. **Do your own "Christian Bar Mitzvah."** Our sons' thirteenth birthday was a special occasion with guests—ministers, family friends, teachers, relatives, and classmates. I took each son to a really nice restaurant for dinner and fellowship with several of my male friends. I wanted him to have friends like these as he grew up. Younger brothers had to wait their turn to enter the **"community of redeemed men."** God wants every father to pull his sons into the community of redeemed men;

> The devil attempts to disqualify and discourage us.

therefore, you must build relationships with other men whom you trust. It takes friends to build community. (Moms can connect daughters with redeemed women.)

Back home we opened presents and pronounced blessings over our child. The blessings, which were written out, along with letters received for the event from friends, were read aloud and later put in a scrapbook. The prayers and celebration made a memorable, special time of "imparting the blessing." We've had positive feedback from our sons' friends and their parents about the impact of these blessing ceremonies.

Each 13th birthday could also be an occasion for sons and daughters to receive a gold ring or necklace as a pledge of virtue and chastity until marriage. This time should be personal—just parent and child.

Blessing our offspring creates opportunities to share the heart of God. We should bless at baptisms, graduations, weddings, promotions, births. Blessing creates a tangible memory of encouragement spoken over our offspring that will remain with them after we are gone.

Even if your kids are grown and out of your home, bless them anyway. They may already have their own family, but they still need to feel your affirmation and encouragement. Call them, drive or fly to meet with them, open your heart to them, and speak faith-filled words of blessing over them. Do it while you have the opportunity.

Say to yourself, "My words have power!" "I will bless and not curse." "I will prosper according to the fruit of my

> God wants every father to pull his sons into the community of redeemed men.

lips." "My words will release the next generation." Say "I bless you in the Name of the Lord," or "I bless you with long life, health, and prosperity," or "I bless you with the blessing of God when He blessed Abraham." Be bold in faith when you bless!

Impart the blessing to your offspring. Do it with an attitude of humility ("Coram Deo"—"before the face of God"). Repent first before God, then ask your children to forgive you. **Then speak "well-words" over them.** There isn't a perfect parent in the whole world. Repentance opens the door, tenderizes the heart, prepares you with humility, and enables the blessing of God to flow through you.

Bless with a Word, a Touch, in Faith and Forever! Put your hand on their shoulder. Hug them. Speak specific words for each child—words of hope, courage, faith. Use faith. Don't wait until they're good enough. Don't keep the blessing just out of reach. You're not a coach—you're a dad. Don't ever revoke the blessing. **Your words have power. God will use you to impact the next generation for His Kingdom!**

Authority to Bless

RELATED SCRIPTURES:
Deuteronomy 30:19-20
Proverbs 6:20-23; 12:14; 13:2; 18:21
Luke 6:28
Ephesians 4:1-7; 6:4
James 3:6, 9-14

APPLICATIONS:
List areas you consider to be your spheres of influence. You may have several (husband, dad, coach, business leader, neighbor, elder, uncle). In each arena, name those whom you have authority to bless.

How do you come into agreement with God so that your words agree with His words about a situation?

Say aloud:

> "My words have power!"

> "I will bless and not curse."

> "I will prosper according to the fruit of my lips."

> "My words will release the next generation."

Write out words of blessing from Scripture, from this book, or from your own thoughts, and determine to actively use them.

PRAYER:

Heavenly Father, I repent for the words I've spoken which cursed, rather than blessed, the hearer. I repent for not making the effort to reflect Your heart through my speech to those around me. I have power to pray and bless in order to accomplish Your purposes. May I speak faith-filled words of blessing so people experience Your grace and come to know You. Thank You, Father, for speaking blessings over me. Amen.

*My words had power to
bring healing to my son.*

Bless the Next Generation

I t was after midnight as I stood quietly in the glow of my two-year-old's nightlight. Once again, the mysterious nighttime cough shook him, robbing him of rest. He was bright, handsome, energetic—the third of four sons. This affliction had lasted over two months, and I was frustrated. Our family doctor had ruled out infection and allergies as the cause. Believing James 5:14 regarding the sick, I'd prayed for him myself as well as had our church elders anoint him with oil and pray for him. There was no improvement. The doctor suggested testing him for a possible genetic lung problem. Tonight, as I stood by his bed, I addressed God again—this time fervently.

"God, I've done what You said, now I want him healed. I want You to heal him tonight." My love for my son and my anger at his condition provoked me to so boldly address God.

I knew God healed today, by natural means, through doctors, and also in answer to believing prayer. As a child, I'd seen miracles when my mother prayed for us kids, and as an adult, I'd experienced answers to prayer. When I was a boy, a serious infection went through the community—people ran fevers and were sick for weeks. I caught it and had a fever of over 103 degrees when Mom called the doctor. He said just to let it run its course, so she called our pastor, who immediately came out to pray for me. He laid hands on me and prayed, but I got worse that night. Mom called him again the next morning, and he returned. He quoted Psalm 103 about God healing all our diseases, and he prayed again—only this time, as he prayed, I broke out in a sweat and began to cool down while his hand still rested on my head—the fever broke, and I recovered that day.

So I knew that God answered prayer and that sometimes we had to pray more than once. Now, my whole heart was interceding to God for my little boy. I stood in the silence that followed my outcry, wondering if, this time, my prayer would be effective.

Down in my belly, in my spirit, I heard God's voice, not audibly, but as an impression that I recognized as being from Him. "Lay your hand on him and bless him." Over the years, I've learned that, most of the time, the voice of God is heard in our belly, where our spirit is, but distracting barbs from the devil are sent against our mind, in our thoughts. I recognized a difference in what God said and what I'd requested—**I was to bless him,** not just ask God to bless him. So I obeyed, laying my hand on my son's head and simply saying, "I bless you in Jesus' Name." The next morning I detected no outward change in our otherwise active, blond-haired, blue-eyed, 100% boy, but his chronic cough never returned. That was many years ago. **Something in my fatherly blessing, done in obedience to the Holy Spirit's prompting, removed the affliction from my son.**

Fathers can influence their children in powerful and crucial ways by either blessing or cursing them with the words of their mouth. "With it we bless our Lord and Father; and with it we curse men ... from the same mouth come both blessing

Read James 3:9-10

THE TONGUE

and cursing. My brethren, these things ought not to be this way" James 3:9-10.

Bless Your WIFE TOO, DON'T CURSE.

Somehow, my words brought about a change in my son's physical condition. We Christians don't bless enough. Parents tend to wait until their kids measure up before blessing them. Leaders tend to wait until their people are perfect before encouraging them. Withholding approval is a common practice with athletic coaches, but it's a damaging habit for parents or leaders. Parents, especially dads, need to bless and affirm their children—sincerely and frequently.

There are plenty of Biblical precedents for imparting blessings. The Patriarchs blessed the generation after them. Abraham blessed Isaac with a covenant command to his servant to take care of Isaac (Genesis 24:1-7; 25:5, 11; 26:24; 28:4). Bethuel and Laban blessed Rebekah with one of the most powerful words in Scripture: "May you, our sister, become thousands of ten thousands, and may your descendants possess the gate of those who hate them" Genesis 24:60. Isaac blessed Jacob: "May God Almighty bless you and make you fruitful and multiply you, that you may become a company of peoples" Genesis 28:3. Jacob blessed Joseph as well as Joseph's sons, Ephraim and Manasseh: "May my name live on in them, and the names of my fathers Abraham and Isaac; and may they grow into a multitude in the midst of the earth" Genesis 48:16. As representatives of God, they spoke powerful words and laid hands on those they blessed. Certainly, their words affected generations after them.

To Bless means

"To bless" means to speak words of life and faith over someone with the intent of positively impacting his or her life. It requires acting on the natural and delegated God-given authority we have as husband, parent, leader, or intercessor.

we CALLED HIM HONEST JOHN.

A parent's words can change a child's self image. Our first, third, and fourth sons had blond hair that attracted a lot of positive attention from strangers. Our second son, a brunette, was either ignored or insensitively asked, "Where's your blond hair?" Walking by his room one day when he was four, I overheard him say to his reflection in the mirror, "I hate you. I hate you, boy with brown hair." He was so intent on venting his hurt that he did not notice me. I sought advice from a father in our church, who shared wise counsel. In the course of our daily routines, we began to speak encouraging words to our son. We told him we loved our brown-haired boy. Instead of just praying for his heart to change, I began to pray over him in a special way—I audibly prayed over him at night, so he could hear me thanking God for my "brown-haired" son. I held him close when I tucked him in bed, and said, "Father, I especially thank You for giving me this handsome son. You have really blessed me with this boy. I am a happy dad!" My wife also began to tell him how much he looked like me, since both of us had brown hair. After a couple of weeks of impromptu casual blessings and heartfelt prayers of gratitude for him, his confidence was restored. The brown hair issue was never mentioned again.

Jesus was blessed. His Father audibly blessed Him as He came up out of the Jordan River after being baptized. Standing there with water running down His face, **He heard His Father's voice from Heaven** say, "This is My beloved Son, in whom I am well pleased" Matthew 3:17. Jesus heard His Father's audible voice on two other occasions while He was ministering (Mark 9:7; John 12:28). He heard it many more times in His Spirit. We all need to hear our Father's voice.

God Blesses Jesus

Jesus chose to humble Himself before John the Baptist, a prophet who was not part of the "established" religion, nor part of the politically acceptable religious movement

of his day. John so thoroughly offended both the religious and political leaders that it eventually cost him his life. The common people were going out to hear John in a popular "grass-roots" revival held on the banks of the river. Jesus went to him and publicly identified with him by submitting to water baptism. If Jesus could humble Himself to be baptized and, in the midst of it, hear His Father audibly speak, we can do the same. Let's become obedient, even to the point of baptism in water, submitting ourselves to anointed hands to plunge us under water, forever burying the old life, and publicly demonstrating the new life we have in Jesus.

What price will we pay to hear our Heavenly Father's words of approval? Will we choose to stay back in town with the prestigious leaders, or will we leave our reputation at the city limits and make our way to the river with the humble and lowly? Will we join those who have heard the prophetic sound proclaim there is something more than organized religion— there's a life-changing, heart-renewing, righteousness-embracing, heavenly invasion going on and whoever is thirsty can come and drink? The crowd at the river is where the action is, where the revelation of the "Lamb of God who takes away the sin of the world" John 1:29 is made known, where people begin to find "a refuge and strength, a very present help in trouble" Psalm 46:1—as Jesus was identified as the Messiah and began His earthly ministry of going about "doing good, and healing all who were oppressed by the devil, for God was with Him" Acts 10:38.

The blessing Jesus received launched Him into ministry. If Jesus, who was perfect, needed His Father's blessing, don't we need it, too? And on a natural level, don't our kids need to hear us speak words of blessing over them? There is a sense in which a child never fully matures until his daddy tells him he's an adult. There must be affirmation from a father figure

God AFFIRMED Jesus (Before) He began his PUBLIC MINISTRY, we Are to do the SAme with our FAm

for a boy to grow into manhood, for a daughter to develop into womanhood. Immediately after Jesus experienced this affirmation from His Father in Heaven, He faced and overcame the devil in the wilderness and entered into His ministry (Matthew 4:1, 11, 17).

The voice Jesus heard from Heaven was accompanied by the presence of the Holy Spirit. The Holy Spirit visibly descended upon Jesus. We need the Holy Spirit, too. We need to be saturated with prayer and be full of God's Spirit, so our blessing over our offspring in the course of the day is accompanied by the presence of God.

Jesus proved Himself faithful in His assignment to become a man, to humble Himself, to learn obedience and patience in His earthly family. God the Father was pleased, and He let His Son know it. But He did this before Jesus was done—Jesus had not yet entered His public ministry, nor had He finished His course and successfully endured the agony of the cross—yet His Heavenly Father affirmed Him and said He was pleased with Him. Furthermore, the Father said it publicly. When it comes to family, affirm publicly and correct privately. God is the pattern Father for us. Don't withhold blessing until your child's obedience is complete and he has proven himself in every arena. Bless now!

> There must be affirmation from a father figure for a boy to grow into manhood, for a daughter to develop into womanhood.

There was a touch involved. Since God is spirit, His touch upon His Son was by the Holy Spirit, who descended upon Jesus as the Father's voice came out of the heavens. We, too, should touch our offspring—hold them, put our hand on their shoulder, put our arm around them—let them feel our affirmation by our words and by our touch.

130

Put your hands on your kids to bless them. Speak positive words over them as you hug them, eat meals with them, play with them, or tuck them into bed at night. Do it regularly. **Don't wait for them to become good enough.** Timing is critical—do it now! Jesus didn't wait for us to become righteous before He died for us on the cross; He blessed unconditionally. Counteract the world's curses of discouragement and doubt with faith-filled blessings. Your words can count forever, just like the Biblical words of blessing by the patriarchs.

You have the power to speak those words! Don't wait on your pastor to bless your family. You are the parent; you bless them! Grandpa, lay hands on your 45-year-old son and bless him. Dad, **bless your children now and often**. Do it while you have the opportunity. Jesus has already made you worthy of the task when He shed His blood for you on the cross.

Blessing your offspring with your words will show them they are loved, it will show them they have value, and it will plant seeds of the Gospel of grace in them that will point them toward their Heavenly Father, who has the best blessing of all for them.

You are not out of your sphere or beyond your authority when you intercede for your family. If God has trusted you with a family, He has trusted you with the authority to bless them. Act in faith to speak words of life in the arena God has given to you. Take your place in the saints' "Hall of Fame." Begin to do what you were called to do—bless the next generation!

> When it comes to family, let's affirm publicly and correct privately.

131

Bless the Next Generation

RELATED SCRIPTURES:
Isaiah 53:4-6
Mark 10:13-16
Luke 24:50
Acts 2:17

APPLICATIONS:
Who has blessed you by speaking words of life and faith to you? How have those words motivated and inspired you? Have they come to pass?

If your father is living, consider asking him to speak words of blessing over you—you may be surprised at the degree of spiritual sensitivity he exercises when he acts within his sphere of authority as a father. If he is not available, maybe there is a father figure who would be willing to bless you.

If the opposite happened—someone predicted failure for you, in effect, spoke curses over you—appeal to God and His provision. It is always appropriate to appeal to a higher authority. Isaiah 53 says Jesus was punished, became cursed, on the cross with the punishment, or curse, due to our disobedience, so we could inherit the blessings of God due Jesus for His sinless obedience. The price has been paid for the curse to be exchanged for a blessing. Ask God to replace those evil words with His Words of blessings.

If there's been no one to bless you, look up Scriptures that speak of the blessings we have received in Christ, and read them aloud to yourself. Repeat this, if necessary, until you begin to believe what those verses say.

Think of people who look to you who might need words of blessing—a son, daughter, grandchild, nephew, niece, or neighbor. It could be someone in your church who doesn't have a caring parent. The blessing is unique and special for each person. How may God use you to release someone from handicapping words?

PRAYER:

Heavenly Father, You blessed me by sending Jesus. He blessed me by dying in my place, paying my debt. Now I can bless others. I break the curses of discouragement and doubt by speaking words of life and faith-filled blessings. Help me positively impact those around me by the words of my mouth. Thank You, Lord God. Amen.

15

> *Develop a three-generation*
> *mind-set at home, in church,*
> *and in business.*

One Generation
Is Not Enough

Although I didn't understand what it meant, when I was fourteen, God called me to fish for men. Part of that calling is to draw men into the Kingdom of God. It is more specific than a general call to the ministry and more fundamental than fulfilling the role of "clergy" (which sounds like a skin disease!), because it touches a man at his identity. It is a call for men to develop a three-generation vision.

FISH FOR MEN,

God spoke to Abram in Genesis 12:1-3, calling him from his homeland to journey to a new land, where, God promised, "I will make you a great nation, and I will bless you, and make your name great; and so you shall be a blessing; ... and in you all of the families of the earth shall be blessed." And so Abram left home. *a Covenant.*

I learned in Bible college that God chose Abram at random, as an act of His sovereign grace. But Genesis 18:19 teaches, "For I have chosen him, so that he may command his children and his household after him to keep the way of the Lord." The King James Version says God chose him **because** He *knew* Abram, knew what he would do, even before he had children.

Does God know you? Does He know what you'll do with the blessings He holds in store for you? Teenager, what does God know about you? What destiny is He waiting to release when He sees your heart is ready?

Abram left his homeland to follow God. Will you move geographically? Will you change jobs for the sake of your family? Will you make the next generation your priority? I have made major moves and job changes at God's leading and for the sake of my family.

Recently, I prayed, "God, You know me; You know what is in my heart." I was surprised to hear that come out of my mouth. But there are places we get in God, where we know what He will do, and He knows what we will do when He answers our request.

GOD TOLD ABRAHAM - YOU WILL POSSESS THE GATES OF HIS ENEMIES

NOT JUST YOUR OWN GATES.

Abraham became the father of our faith (Romans 4:16) and is a model for us. In Genesis 22:17, God promised this father, "Indeed I will greatly bless you ... and your seed shall possess the gate of their enemies." We might think it would be enough to preserve the gates of our own cities, families, churches, businesses, but God promised Abraham that he would control his enemies' points of power—the places of access, communication, commerce, culture, and wealth. **When there is a man around who has a multi-generational vision, his enemies' gates are in jeopardy!**

> **What destiny is He waiting to release when He sees your heart is ready?**

What are your gates? Has your family been poor for generations? Are you locked out of prosperity? Have you lacked the training or education required to prosper and gain influence? Has your family been plagued with divorce or alcoholism? **These points of control need to be taken and held for the Kingdom of God.**

What about our society's gates? Can we change the Supreme Court by asking God to remove justices who have passed or supported wicked laws? Go after the media who control TV and movies? Revamp the education system? Redeem business, government, and the arts? What gates are in place, and how many generations will it take to capture them?

This isn't just for men. God also has an awesome promise for girls and mothers as seen in Genesis 24:60. Rebekah's brother Laban and father Bethuel prayed over and blessed her before sending her off to be Isaac's bride. "May you, our sister, become thousands of ten thousands, and may your descendants possess the gate of those who hate them." What a promise! **What if you knew that you would inherit the place of power and access of those who hate and despise you?** What favor God placed on Rebekah!

The promise to control the gates of your enemies is always found in the context of more than one generation. It transcends generations. "I will establish My covenant between Me and you and your descendants" Genesis 17:7. Some things are just too big for one generation to accomplish.

> The promise to control the gates of your enemies is always found in the context of more than one generation.

King David prepared the supplies for the temple he wanted to build, but God told him Solomon was to build it. As a faithful steward, David left the supplies for Solomon, but David left even more. He also gave his son the design—the blueprints

God had revealed to him for the temple (1 Chronicles 28:11). Let's not just lay up stuff for our kids—let's also leave them a vision, a plan, a target.

Part of the plan for our descendants is for them to pass on the same vision. It could be possible for all the descendants after us to follow Jesus until He returns. Some of the dreams to affect our society are so big—or came so late in life—we need to pass them to the next crew to finish. **Successfully doing business until He returns (Luke 19:11-13) requires implementing a multi-generational strategy.**

Jonathon Edwards, born in 1703, was the pastor in Northampton, Massachusetts, where the First Great Awakening broke out in the American colonies. From there, revival swept through the territories, preparing the way for the formation of the character of our about-to-be-birthed United States. Jonathon Edwards, called America's greatest theologian, spent an hour each day with his children, even though he daily prayed and studied for hours. He and his wife had eleven children. A study begun in 1887 identified 1394 decendants. Among them were 100 lawyers, 20 judges, 13 college presidents, over 100 college professors, 60 physicians, several military chaplains, 75 officers of the Army and Navy, over 100 pastors, missionaries, and theologians, 60 authors of over 135 books, 3 United States Senators, 1 Chaplain of the Senate, 80 public servants such as mayors and governors, and one Vice President of the United States. In addition, many were officers or presidents of companies in fields such as railways, banks, insurance, and production of coal, iron, oil, and silver.[1]

> Successfully "occupying until He comes" requires implementing a multi-generational strategy.

138

Read

In contrast, there was a contemporary of Edwards, Max Jukes [fictitious name]. In 1874, Richard Dugdale, performing research for the New York Prison Commission, discovered descendants of Jukes in 6 different New York prisons, prompting further study. Of the 540 direct descendants and 1200 relatives found—spanning 5 generations—310 were paupers for a collective duration of 2300 years. Seven were murderers, 60 were thieves, and 130 were convicted of lesser crimes. Three hundred of the 1200 died in infancy, and many of the women were prostitutes. Only 20 learned a trade, and 10 of those learned the trade in prison. The Jukes were, for the most part, either paupers or criminals.[2] **What you and I do with our lives has a profound effect upon subsequent generations.**

A father can impact his descendants, even those whom he never meets. G.W. McCluskey prayed for his family from 11:00 am to noon every day. Later in his life, he began to pray for his children's descendants. A few weeks before his death, G.W. amazed his associates by saying God had promised him that all the descendants after him for four generations would be believers. In fact, all these descendants either became ministers or married ministers—except one—Dr. James Dobson, founder of Focus on the Family, a fourth generation, Jesus-serving descendant of a praying parent.[3]

Decide to pray for your family. Decide to bless your family. Decide to provide for your family. You can make a difference. And if you become a man whom God knows, whom He can bless, then this promise to Abraham will also be yours—**"Do not fear, Abram, I am a shield to you; Your reward shall be very great"** Genesis 15:1.

"Do the stuff!"

[1] A. E. Winship, Litt. D., *Jukes-Edwards, A Study in Education and Heredity*, (Harrisburg, PA: R. L. Myers & Co., 1990,) pp. 28-31.

[2] *Ibid.*, pp. 7-8.

[3] Dr. James Dobson, *When God Doesn't Make Sense*, (Wheaton, IL: Tyndale House Publishers, Inc., 1992), pp. 202-203.

One Generation Is Not Enough

RELATED SCRIPTURES:
Genesis 1:28
Deuteronomy 6:2, 3, 7, 8
Deuteronomy 11:19-26
Deuteronomy 12:28-31

APPLICATIONS:
In light of God's instructions to Adam, how do you know God was thinking of many generations?

How many generations are we commanded to train to fear the Lord?

How important are fathers and grandfathers in God's plans?

Who has primary responsibility for your children's instruction?

What role do church leaders play?

Who is the primary trainer, coach, mentor, and teacher of the next generation?

How do you bond with the generation after you?

PRAYER:

Heavenly Father, You have disciplined me as a son. You have placed Your Spirit within me. I submit my spirit to Your Spirit. Fill me with Your heart, the heart of a father. Let the next generation after me reap the benefits of Your mercy upon me. I will speak words of life to my sons and daughters. I will tell them of Your awesome deeds and our deliverance through Jesus. I will tell them of the spiritual warfare that rages around us so they can be delivered from this present evil age into Your Kingdom. May my home be filled with the atmosphere of Your home, so they get a taste of Heaven on earth. I pray, in Jesus' Name. Amen.

16

Associating with anointed men of God impacts us and the generations after us.

Riding with Jehu

The forces of Jezebel, working in the household of Ahab, almost destroyed the spiritual heritage in Israel. The same evil powers work today to wound, delay, or kill emerging male leadership in God's church. As long as the church is passive, bound, and ineffectual, the enemy wins. **It takes the restoration of the prophets to complete the restoration of men.**

Jeremiah called the sons of Jonadab, son of Rechab, and offered them wine (Jeremiah 35:2-11). They refused, saying their father Jonadab had instructed them never to own land, plant fields, build houses, or drink wine. They had lived in tents until invading armies forced them to flee into Jerusalem, but they still held to their father's instructions to avoid wine. They had made a vow before God. In other places in Scripture, similar vows were called "Nazirite vows." Typically, they were made for a period of time, for the purpose of prayer, and usually involved giving up some legitimate pleasure or food for a season. However, this vow

> It takes the restoration of the prophets to complete the restoration of men.

had lasted into the next generation. Even God was impressed. He said, "Because you have obeyed the command of Jonadab your father ... (he) shall not lack a man to stand before Me always" Jeremiah 35:18, 19.

Jeremiah asked, "If the sons of Jonadab would keep their father's commands, why wouldn't the nation of Israel keep its Heavenly Father's commands?"

God used the obedience of the Rechabites as an object lesson to set in motion judgment upon the disobedient in Israel (Jeremiah 35:16-17). In the same way, **God will use the obedience of the church as the key to bring judgment upon the unbelievers** (2 Corinthians 10:6).

God promised blessings to the descendants of Jonadab because they were faithful to the words left to them (Jeremiah 35:18-19). Blessings will be ours as well for the same kind of faithfulness.

Why did these sons of Jonadab, Rechab's son, keep their father's words long after he died? What was the secret of their obedience to the old man's instructions?

Would we obey instructions from our father or grand-father? The words we give our offspring today may seem as strange as the words left to Rechab's grandsons. Our warnings against drugs, the addictive nature of pornography, or the dangers of dabbling in the occult may seem as unusual to our children as the instructions given to the Rechabites. After all, "the other kids at school are doing these things."

But the distinction between our current instructions and those past commands is even more extreme because what Jonadab told his sons had nothing to do with sin; he gave them instructions regarding abstaining from what were normal and wholesome activities. It would be like telling our children never to own a car or drink carbonated beverages.

It is a tremendous task to so clearly convey a vision that it is received and acted upon. Think of any major change in a corporate business structure and all the training and re-training necessary to get everyone moving together in the new direction. Something at work in Jonadab caused his instructions to be imparted to the next generation in a powerful, lasting way. Only one story about Jonadab is recorded in Scripture. It has to be the key that enabled Jonadab to impart his message so that it took hold.

God anointed Jehu to destroy all the house of Ahab (2 Kings 9). Elisha called one of the sons of the prophets and sent him to pour a flask of oil on the head of Jehu, anointing him to become King of Israel.

Riding to Jezreel to fulfill his mission, Jehu found Joram, the ruling King of Israel, and killed him in Naboth's vineyard, which Ahab, Joram's father, had previously stolen. Jehu also killed Ahaziah, King of Judah, who was visiting Joram. In Jezreel, Jehu ordered Jezebel to be thrown off her balcony, and he then trampled her body under his horse's hooves. He sent word to the elders of Samaria who guarded Ahab's other sons and ordered the boys' heads to be delivered in baskets. The seventy sons were executed. Then Jehu killed the forty-two relatives of Ahaziah who were coming to greet Jezebel's offspring. But Jehu wasn't finished.

On his way to destroy the prophets of Baal, he passed Jonadab, son of Rechab, and invited him to ride in his chariot. "He greeted him, and said to him, 'Is your heart right, as my heart is with your heart?' And Jonadab answered, 'It is.' Jehu said, 'If it is, give me your hand.' And he gave him his hand, and he took him up to him into the chariot. And he said, 'Come with me, and see my zeal for the Lord.' So he made him ride in his chariot. And when he came to Samaria, he killed all who remained to Ahab in Samaria, until he had destroyed him, according to the word of the Lord, which He spoke to Elijah" 2 Kings 10:15-17.

Then Jehu gathered all the prophets of Baal and slaughtered them, instructing his men, "the one who permits any of the men whom I bring into your hands to escape, shall give up his life in exchange" 2 Kings 10:24.

Jonadab rode with Jehu! Jehu's anointing to fulfill the prophetic word affected Jonadab. He was pulled into the conflict, rode into battle, and was somehow imparted with Jehu's courage and power. Being in the middle of the battle affected Jonadab for life. He saw for himself the judgment of God upon witchcraft, immorality, and abuse of authority. Jonadab was never the same.

Because he rode with Jehu, Jonadab was so energized that, when he spoke to his children, he was still empowered and motivated. His conviction so moved his offspring that, even after he was gone, they honored his instructions and kept his word.

We men need to "ride with Jehu" in order to motivate our offspring to keep the word of the Lord. We need to feel the fierceness of the battle, see the blood on our Captain's sword, and experience the victory over oppressive forces that have enslaved us. We need to remember the sounds of battle as well as the shouts of victory.

Jesus is our Jehu! His victory over Satan is our victory as well. Jesus is the Captain of the hosts of the armies of God. He is riding against the tyranny of enslaving sin and demoralizing attacks on God's people. On the way to the battle, He asks if our heart is right, and if it is, He pulls us into His chariot to give us a taste of victory.

It is here, riding with our Captain, that we are empowered to motivate the generations after us. The battle is fierce, the struggle is epic, but the victory is awesome!

Just as the prophet Elisha called forth the Jehu ministry, so **today's prophetic ministry will bring a fresh revelation of Jesus.** "For the testimony of Jesus is the spirit of prophecy" Revelation 19:10. The restoration of the prophetic today foretells a coming **victory over the forces of witchcraft and tyranny** that have oppressed the church. A new day of liberty is coming! The fully functioning prophetic ministry restores manliness and godliness.

The priestly intercessors, driven from their place and forced to return to the fields (2 Chronicles 11:14), will return to the house of the Lord. The prophets, removed by the substitute religions attempting to silence the voice of God, will again be heard, bringing the word of the Lord to the common people. Prosperity will return as God's judgment is lifted from the land.

> The prophetic ministry functioning in the church restores manliness and godliness to the church.

May the Lord, who wants us to pull our sons into the community of redeemed men, pull us into His chariot and so equip us with a taste of victory that we cannot fail to pass the vision to the next generation. **Let's be ready to answer when He asks if our heart is with Him.**

"Come, let us return to the Lord. For He has torn us, but He will heal us; He has wounded us, but He will bandage us ... So let us know, let us press on to know the Lord. His going forth is as certain as the dawn" Hosea 6:1, 3.

Let's do the stuff!

Riding with Jehu

RELATED SCRIPTURES:
Mark 9:2-8
Acts 3, 4, especially 4:13
Hebrews 13:7

APPLICATIONS:
Peter and John caused quite an uproar because a lame man was healed (Acts 3:6). Why do you think this miracle happened to Peter and John?

What types of victories did Peter and John observe while Jesus was with them? What was the impact on the disciples who were afterwards born into the Kingdom?

DR SIMON

Are you hanging around leaders who demonstrate only patience and tolerance for demonic strongholds, or are you hanging with leaders who take action and go to war? Knowing you will become like the ones with whom you associate, what are your thoughts about prophetic and apostolic mentors in addition to teaching and pastoral role models?

Patience may be a virtue, but avoiding war when it is called for is cowardice and laziness. Is God calling you to change the culture around you? Has God sent a word and a fresh anointing to you?

Could there be some junior, unnamed prophet already waiting to catch you alone to deliver to you a message from God? Could God directly speak a fresh word to you? What would you do with such a word?

Plan significant prayer times so you can receive impartation from Jesus.

PRAYER:
Heavenly Father, You have sent Jesus, the Mighty Warrior, the Captain of Your army, to wage war against the spirits of witchcraft that hold men in bondage. May I feel His strength, His sweat, His anger, His hand clenched around His sword as He pulls me into the battle beside Him. Give me a measure of the anointing on Jesus, my Jehu. May I never be the same. May I be so transformed by the battle experience with Jesus that I receive a fresh level of authority to lead my family and the descendants after me. Jesus, You are my Captain. I give You my allegiance. I long to be with You in battle, that You not have to go alone. I long to be with You in the victory celebrations and in the establishment of Your peaceful reign on earth. Even as David had his mighty warriors standing with him, may I be privileged to stand with You! In Your Name, I pray. Amen.

17

*We must be mindful of our
descendants and the effects
of our lives upon them.*

GOOD CHAPTER —
MABY THE BEST.

Residue of the Covenant

P uritan preacher John Cotton said it was "evident by the light of nature, that all civil relations are founded in covenant."[1] As Governor of the Massachusetts Bay Colony in 1630, John Winthrop established terms of covenant as the spiritual and social bonds of their new community, doing so with the recognition of providence and God's law as the context. Covenant life is not just commitment to one another as a mere social contract, but it is **commitment to live with one another in the light of God's revealed will and in His presence.**

Read

The covenant glue that holds society together begins with God's law. It is seen in the marriage covenant. "The Lord has been a witness between you and the wife of your youth, against whom you have dealt treacherously, though she is your companion and your wife by covenant" Malachi 2:14.

God desires offspring. He has desired a people since the time He placed Adam in the garden. **The Ten Commandments promise multigenerational curses and blessings.** "For I, the Lord your God, am a jealous God, visiting the iniquity of the fathers on the children, and on the third and the

INIQUITY TO 4th GENERATION,
LOVINGING KINDNESS TO A thousand generations

"fourth generations of those who hate Me, but showing lovingkindness to thousands, to those who love Me and keep My commandments" Deuteronomy 5:9, 10.

The covenant blessing extends to descendants of obedient families. "The Lord your God, He is God, the faithful God, who keeps His covenant and His lovingkindness to a thousandth generation with those who love Him and keep His commandments" Deuteronomy 7:9.

Again and again, **the mercy of God has fallen on people because of God's promises to their forefathers.** "The Lord did not set His love on you nor choose you because you were more in number than any of the peoples, for you were the fewest of all peoples, but because the Lord loved you and kept the oath which He swore to your forefathers, the Lord brought you out by a mighty hand, and redeemed you" Deuteronomy 7:7, 8. **God keeps covenant with families!**

This is not an Old Testament truth, but a Biblical truth. Mary prophesied, "His mercy is upon generation after generation toward those who fear Him ... He has given help ... to Abraham and his offspring forever" Luke 1:50, 54, 55.

God answers the prayers of godly parents for their offspring. Consider the widow's son. "Now as He approached the gate of the city, behold, a dead man was being carried out, the only son of his mother, and she was a widow; and a sizable crowd from the city was with her. And when the Lord saw her, He felt compassion for her, and said to her, 'Do not weep.' And He came up and touched the coffin; and the bearers came to a halt. And He said, 'Young man, I say to you, arise!' And the dead man sat up, and began to speak. And Jesus gave him back to his mother" Luke 7:12-15. There is no record of the son's faith or prayers. **This was for the mother.**

A father came and asked for help for his demonized son. "'Teacher, I beg You to look at my son, for he is my only boy, and behold, a spirit seizes him ...' And while he was still approaching, the demon dashed him to the ground, and threw him into a violent convulsion. But Jesus rebuked the unclean spirit, and healed the boy, and gave him back to his father" Luke 9:38, 39, 42. There is no evidence that the boy was able to call on God. **This was for the father.**

The daughter of the synagogue official was sick. Her father, Jairus, fell at Jesus' feet and implored Him to come to his house. On the way, a servant met them and said the girl had died. Jesus told the parent, "Do not be afraid any longer; only believe, and she shall be made well" Luke 8:50. Arriving at her home, He "took her by the hand and called, saying, 'Child, arise!' And her spirit returned, and she rose up immediately ... And her parents were amazed" Luke 8:54-56. The little girl wasn't able to pray. **This was for the parents.**

When parents call upon God, the result is mercy and grace upon the generations following after them. While it is true that each generation must seek after God, **God predisposes mercy toward the descendants of godly, praying parents. We must be mindful of our descendants and the effects our lives have upon them.** "See that you do not despise one of these little ones, for I say to you, that their angels in Heaven continually behold the face of My Father who is in Heaven. ... Thus it is not the will of your Father who is in Heaven that one of these little ones perish" Matthew 18:10, 14.

Take confidence. **You and your children are the beneficiaries of your ancestors' intercession.** If your children are weak or

> When parents call upon God, the result is mercy and grace upon the generations following after them.

have been taken captive by the enemies of God, intercede for them in faith that your prayers will work. As priest over your home, you have authority with God. You are in your rightful role as head of your home and spiritual forerunner of the next generation. Go ahead—take your place in the faith-fight. Intercede in the night hours. Proclaim the promises of God over your offspring. And, in faith, when you have heard from God, **prophesy to your sons and daughters.** Don't use religious language; **speak faith-filled words into their spirit** when you are hugging them, encouraging them, or even writing to them. Have confidence that the favor of God is multigenerational in its outworking.

You and I reap the benefits of Jesus' death on the cross as well as experience the effects of our forefathers' obedience to God. Mercy triumphs over judgment. While the curse extends three or four generations, the favor of God extends a thousand generations! Covenant has multigenerational implications. **The effects of receiving covenant with God through the work of Christ on the cross extend into the next generation** and draw that generation to the God of their fathers. This is another reason why **it is vital that fathers turn their hearts toward their children** (Malachi 4:6).

There is a residual blessing that remains. "And Elisha died, and they buried him. Now the bands of the Moabites would invade the land in the spring of the year. And as they were burying a man, behold, they saw a marauding band; and they cast the man into the grave of Elisha. And when the man touched the bones of Elisha he revived and stood up on his feet" 2 Kings 13:20, 21.

Neither the dead soldier nor Elisha was exercising faith at that moment, but something remained after Elisha was gone! We may not have the gift of miracles like Elisha, but there is a residual anointing where we have been that quickens those after us. **God wants to touch a generation of wounded soldiers.** Our lowest point, where we were laid, as it were in death, may be the place of anointing to deliver the next generation.

It's not you, but it's His power, working through the generations according to the promise of the Covenant. His word is true. He has bound Himself with an oath to all the believing descendants of Abraham. "'By Myself I have sworn,' declares the Lord ... 'indeed I will greatly bless you ... and in your descendants all the nations of the earth shall be blessed'" Genesis 22:16-18. He has sealed the covenant and demonstrated His faithfulness to fulfill His word in the death and resurrection of His own Son on the cross at Calvary.

> Our lowest point, where we were laid, as it were in death, may be the place of anointing to deliver the next generation.

Today, **there is a promise of blessing for you as you look to Him in faith**—a promise as sure as the resurrection of Christ from the grave. It is a promise for you, with residual blessings for the generations after you!

[1]Ken Meyers, *Tabletalk*, August 1995, "On Contracts and Covenants," p. 59.

Residue of the Covenant

RELATED SCRIPTURES:
Exodus 34:7
Leviticus 26:44, 45
Deuteronomy 4:9
1 Chronicles 16:15
Psalms 78:1-4; 103:17, 18; 105:8; 112:1, 2; 132:12
Proverbs 17:6; 20:7
Isaiah 44:3

APPLICATIONS:
"Covenant life is a commitment to live with one another in the light of God's revealed will and in His presence." If you believe this is true, what adjustments should you make in your present relationships?

What multigenerational curses or blessings has your family experienced?

How do you change the cycle of failure to a pattern of success?

Write out the promises God has made to you for your offspring.

Pray these promises over your offspring.

Intercede in prayer for children in your life who don't have praying parents. Speak faith-filled words over them. (Realize that there are 30, 40, and 50-year-old "children" who also need this type of intercession.)

Pray that "He will turn the hearts of the fathers to their children, and the hearts of the children to their fathers" Malachi 4:6. This means turn your heart toward your children. If your parents are still living, also turn your heart to them.

PRAYER:
Heavenly Father, thank You for Your promises. Thank You for being the God of healing and restoration. Father, I determine to be a godly, praying parent. I commit to live in such a way that my life positively impacts my family. Lord, break the cycle of generational curses from us. Dispel the darkness and enable us to become a mighty force to spread the light of the Gospel of Jesus Christ into our spheres of influence. Thank You, Father. Amen.

FATHERPOWER®
Ministries International

Suggested uses for

father**POWER**®

Generational Leadership

Individual Study

Personal Evangelistic Tool

Family Devotions

Reconnecting with Adult Children

Sunday School

Home School/Private School Curriculum

Men's Ministry

Parenting Class

Business Development Focus Group Study

Leadership Training Curriculum

Church Planting Strategy Resource

Prison Ministry Resource

Graduates, Newlyweds, New Parents, Servicemen

Let us know the impact this book
has on your life!
~ *Don and Kay Wood*

To order additional copies or to contact us:

MPower Publishing
P.O. Box 1201
Bedford, TX 76095-1201

www.fatherpower.com